The Healthy Habit Revolution:

Your Step-by-Step Blueprint to Create Better Habits in 5 Minutes a Day

By Derek Doepker

Published by Doepker Global LLC

200 E Broadway 355

Glendale, CA 91205

The Healthy Habit Revolution: Create Better Habits in 5 Minutes a Day by Derek Doepker —2nd edition.

ISBN

Paperback: 978-1-7323456-0-7

Disclaimer:

Editor: Marjorie Kramer - Marjorie.Kramer@gmail.com

CONTENTS

Introduction

Do you want to know…

- How you can permanently improve your habits in all areas of life in only five minutes a day without ever feeling overwhelmed?
- What perspective makes it impossible to develop lasting habits unless it's changed *first*?
- How to develop "too-easy-to-fail" habits that guarantee success every day?
- What force is stronger than willpower?
- How the wrong type of reward can actually sap your motivation?
- Why you need to both simplify *and* complicate things to be successful?
- What sports fans can teach you about creating better habits?

Before I go any further, you may be wondering who I am and what makes me qualified to teach this stuff. While I'm currently a bestselling author, fitness coach, and trainer to entrepreneurs, I didn't start out this way.

My journey began when I was 17 years old. I was eating fast food every single night, never exercised, was terribly unhealthy, and no one could have paid me to change. Then, I discovered a few insights which you'll learn later, that allowed me to do a complete 180, get myself into great shape, and most importantly, reprogram my habits so I maintained a fit body for 11 years straight without requiring any great feats of willpower on my part.

After transforming my fitness habits, however, I started to notice just how difficult it was to get those same results in other areas of my life. Have you ever had the experience of having it totally together in one area of your life while other things seem to be falling apart? While my body was great, others habits relating to my finances, social life, and overall happiness needed a lot of work.

I would wonder, why was I able to change some habits and not others? I was also extremely disappointed when, after sharing great fitness tips with my friends who asked for help, most of them wouldn't change a single thing they were doing. Imagine how frustrating it is to offer the best advice in the world only to have it fall on deaf ears. I wanted to help those I cared about, but obviously I was missing something.

Then I got curious. I wasn't forced to change my fitness habits because I hit rock bottom. Rather, I changed my habits almost overnight by what seemed to be a simple conscious choice to better my life. Yet when I looked around, I saw so many people who were making grand New Year's resolutions and setting big goals, but who struggled to make lasting change. Some friends and family members seemed desperate to change things, and yet no amount of motivation they had ever lasted long enough for them to make any type of lasting change.

Was I able to change some of my habits because I was more disciplined and stronger willed, or did I just do something a little differently than most people? I realized that if it was my *strategy* rather than my personality that was responsible for my success, I could show people how to change their long-standing habits without having to wait until things got so bad that they were *forced* to change. I could also apply the strategies to other key areas of my life that I wanted to improve.

This led me to start studying everything I could about psychology, motivation, and personal development to get to the bottom of why we do what we do. I wanted to know how you can reprogram your brain for more creativity, drive, and success in almost any area of life. It turns out, there were a few simple but profound reasons why some people change and others don't. I saw that there is a blueprint for human behavior that, once understood, allows you to create dramatic transformations in your habits. With this information, I learned how to "hack the brain" so to speak. It turns out, you're not doomed to be a victim of your current habits, traits, and personality. Research has shown that we are far more flexible and adaptable than previously thought. Pretty sweet huh?

Once I saw the dramatic results in my own life by applying what I had learned, I decided to pass that information on to others so they could achieve the same benefits without having to spend years researching this information.

Many of the strategies and insights that I'm sharing in this book are from people much smarter than me who have studied habits and human behavior extensively. What I did was distill down their knowledge to make it easy for me to remember and, most importantly, apply. Now I'm sharing that simplified knowledge with you so you can upgrade your own habits the *smart way* – which you'll learn doesn't require superhuman willpower or hyped-up motivation.

While you'll see plenty of personal examples from my life, realize that the underlying principles I'm applying aren't just something I made up. Instead, the lessons and insights shared here come from my research into the psychology of habit development. What I've done is simplify the concepts into actionable steps you can take. There are recommended resources at the end of this book for those who also want an objective, scientific explanation behind many of these concepts as well as reading about other people's experiences applying these techniques.

This book is primarily about *subtraction* rather than addition. By subtracting out all the fluff and giving you just a single thing or two to focus on each day, you'll naturally move forward to make huge breakthroughs almost effortlessly.

While I may be adding some new ideas and concepts to your knowledge, I bet there will be a lot of things in this book that fall under the common sense category. So why is this book so critically important if you want to change your habits? What I've found most people need to change isn't *more* information on how to change. If anything, people are often overwhelmed with too much information and that *keeps* them from progressing. What you need instead is a *step-by-step blueprint* that takes all the thought out of it. Changing habits can be hard enough as it is. Wouldn't you prefer something that makes the entire process a no-brainer?

It's also important to understand there are a few things about human behavior and habit development that are completely counterintuitive, or at the very least, rarely talked about. For instance, there's a single trait that, if you don't cultivate it, will make long-term habit change virtually impossible. My goal with writing this book is to fill in the gaps many other people leave out.

It's also essential to learn the aspects of changing your habits as part of a holistic system. While you can get great results with some isolated tactics here and there, this book is about creating something greater than the sum of its parts. Learning something like the micro-habits approach is great, but it's not enough unless you combine it with other crucial principles. As you'll discover when you get to the end of the book, I've also planted a few hidden lessons that can dramatically increase your happiness and success far beyond simply developing better habits.

Ready to get started? Keep reading to find out how you can use this book to transform your habits in only five minutes a day.Download Your Daily Action Guide

Download Your Daily Action Guide

Download and print your daily action guide by visiting:
http://upgradeyourhabits.com/guide

Using This Book

This is a no-fluff book designed to show you how to improve habits without wasting a lot of time. I cut the word count down significantly to make sure each chapter can be read within a few minutes and that you can get on with *applying* the information as soon as possible. There will be additional recommended reading in the resources section for when you want to take things even further.

This is a 21-day challenge, where each day should take you approximately five minutes to complete the action steps at the end of each chapter. During your very first time through the challenge, it may take more than five minutes on some days. As you get familiar with the process however, you'll find you'll get through the daily action steps much quicker.

You'll also pick a habit that only takes a couple minutes a day to do *at most*. You can even pick a habit that only takes you a few seconds. If you're trying to get in the habit of say, meditating for 30 minutes a day, don't worry. You can still strive for that if you want and this book will help, but the bare minimum might be meditating for 30 *seconds* a day while going through this challenge. Pretty easy, right?

This also means whenever I refer to "your habit" or "your healthy habit," I'm referring to the particular habit you're working on in this book. You'll stick with one single habit you'd like to really focus on for the next 21 days, so you don't get overwhelmed with trying to change too many things at once.

While 21 days is typically how long it's been said that it takes for something to become a habit, in reality it can take a lot longer than 21 days for a habit to become fixed. What I've done, though, is make sure you develop the *foundation* for a lasting habit in 21 days. You'll still need to keep up with the daily actions outlined in this book, which only take a few minutes a day after the 21 days is over to ensure your new habit gets programmed into your subconscious mind.

This also means that it's not ideal to skip ahead to keep things easy. While I can't fault you for being so captivated by my incredible words of wisdom that you want to read more, reading *without* applying the action steps for the day won't get you anywhere. It's like reading how to drive a car better without actually getting behind the wheel. Don't you think you'd get better at driving by actually doing some driving? If you find yourself wishing to read more, then I suggest checking out the bonus chapters in the back of the book.

Another issue for some people is they deal with my greatest nemesis, the "all or nothing" mentality. If you're like me, you may not always want to do just some tiny little action each day. I typically want to go all out and hit huge goals *fast*. If you're that way, I get it. You're a high achiever, and that's amazing. The problem is that, while this works for some things, habit development is a very gradual process. If you're still interested in how you can get dramatic results fast, on day 21 I'll reveal a powerful approach to creating breakthroughs in your life in a very short time frame.

Finally, we come to what may be the most important foundational characteristic responsible for success in developing your habits. If you get nothing else out of this book, understanding the difference between two fundamentally different mindsets will give you a look into why some succeed and others struggle.

This difference is described by Carol Dweck as either a growth mindset or a fixed mindset. Individuals with a growth mindset value learning and personal development. They see mistakes as opportunities to get helpful feedback. They also see their characteristics, including their habits, as things that can be changed and improved upon with practice. Those with a fixed mindset, however, see changing themselves to any significant degree as nearly impossible. This means their self-esteem is reliant upon only seeing positive results and avoiding failure at all costs.

Keep in mind that this is a spectrum, so people don't strictly fall into one mindset or another. I was talking to a woman who believed that people *can* change, but she thought she was too old and set in her ways, thereby making the process of growth seem nearly impossible. While she didn't have a completely fixed mindset, she was just far enough on that side of the spectrum that she would have to break that mindset *first* before any real progress could be made.

If you're reading this book, you probably have at least a little bit of a growth mindset. Otherwise, you'd scoff at a book that claims it can help you change your habits. However, realize you can always cultivate your growth mindset *even more*. Tomorrow, you'll be discovering a way to help create this shift to naturally go deeper into a growth mindset.

If at any point you're finding yourself having trouble moving forward because of not being sure if you have the perfect plan, you're wrestling with all-or-nothing type thinking, or you're unsure you can grow because you've developed more of a fixed mindset, my suggestion is to ask yourself, "Can I just give it a shot and treat my first time through this like a *practice* run?" If you approach it like you're just practicing and having fun with it, you won't put the pressure on yourself to be perfect. Plus, wouldn't you like to have fun with the process?

Remember that at first, *practice is more important than performance*. Once you have a routine established, *then* you can focus on getting better results. You can always run through the 21-day program again with all the kinks ironed out.

It can also be helpful, especially for those working to overcome a fixed mindset, to take on the one characteristic that can create change before you have belief in yourself. That characteristic is *curiosity*. Even if you don't believe dramatic change is possible, you can still make progress if you're curious enough to just see what happens. You may think, "What if it actually works? I don't know if I believe this or not, but I wonder what will happen if I try it out. I guess I'll give it a shot just to satisfy my curiosity."

Additionally, you can always email me with questions at derek@ upgradeyourhabits.com if you *really* get stuck. Yeah, I'm pretty awesome like that where I'll help you out. #yourewelcome

Ready to get started? Your first step is to download the daily action guide and print it out. Alternatively, you can simply just get some blank pieces of paper ready. There will be writing activities throughout the days, and I recommend writing your answers *by hand* on a piece of paper. Writing by hand gets more of your brain involved.

Next, schedule a time each day to read the daily chapters. I suggest first thing in the morning before anything else distracts you. I've kept the chapters short enough so that they only take a few minutes to read. Create a reminder or set the book where you'll see it to remember to read it each day.

Then, think of a reward for completing this challenge. What's something special you can do for yourself? Pick something you'll be excited about. You'll give this to yourself only after completing the challenge. I've also included a reward for you at the end of this book if you email me your results of the challenge to show you've completed it.

Once you've printed the daily action guide (or gotten your paper ready), have set up a system so you remember to read this book each day, and thought of a reward, you're done for today! Just three steps. I told you this was going to be easy, right? Congratulate yourself on being so awesome by starting the journey to healthy habits!

Day 1: Why You Can't Change Habits Until You Change This First

"We are what we repeatedly do. Excellence, then, is not an act, but a *habit*." - *Aristotle*

There's one thing that will sabotage your success from the start if you're not aware of it. You can apply every practice in this book or any other methods of habit change, but there's a good chance you'll fall back into old patterns of behavior sooner or later if you're not aware of this one thing.

That one thing is simply this - *How you define success.*

In our goal-oriented society, success is usually associated with a tangible positive result. For instance, is a person more likely to be congratulated for eating a salad every day for lunch *or* congratulated for losing 50 pounds? Even though switching their usual lunch to a salad may have been a big key to their weight loss, we typically only see, and therefore recognize, the end result and not the mundane things that were behind achieving it.

More importantly, do you congratulate *yourself* for your daily actions, or do you only feel a sense of accomplishment only after reaching a big milestone? Or, have you ever done everything right, but beat yourself up because you didn't see the results you wanted?

This is critically important because habits, as you'll learn, are built from *repeated* emotional rewards including a feeling of accomplishment. The more often you feel successful, the more likely you are to *do* what made you feel successful. Success breeds even more success.

If you don't feel rewarded by doing small steps and making gradual improvements, then you'll rarely stick with something long enough to feel the accomplishment of a big payoff.

Part of the reason I developed the skills I have as a guitar player is because I enjoyed the learning process of practicing guitar. While it wasn't always fun, the small improvements I saw each time I played the guitar were rewarding enough to reinforce the behavior of daily practice. The same could be said about going to the gym, eating healthier foods, and even flossing. These things weren't always habits for me, and in some cases I downright avoided them. Yet they managed to become habits when I learned to associate the behaviors with a positive feeling *each time* I did them. It takes too long to see big results from these things externally, so the reward *initially had to come from within.*

When I think of the epitome of enjoying a process and not having any particular desire for an outcome, I think of dancing. Dancing is moving the body without an intent to go anywhere. All of the movement is done for the simple enjoyment of the movement itself.

On the flip side, a big reason people have trouble getting started with a healthy habit is that they fear failure, a sign of being too far into a fixed mindset rather than a growth mindset. We're generally more motivated to avoid pain than to gain pleasure. If, in the back of a person's mind, they feel like they won't be successful, they'll often find ways to avoid getting started in order to avoid feeling like a failure.

As counterintuitive as it seems, one of the best ways to overcome an outcome-dependent mentality is by looking at the *outcome* of that mentality. Since you're reading this book, you're probably savvy enough to understand that most of the outcomes you have in your life at this moment are a result of the habits you've had for the past few years. That means if you want to see the value in changing your habits, we need to do a little trick with your mind's perspective in today's action steps. I should warn you though, if you're not happy with your current results, showing you the harsh truth of what you're doing to yourself could be a little painful. So ask yourself, "Would I rather trade a little pain now for a lot less pain down the road?"

Recap

- How you define success will determine *when* you feel successful.
- Habits are built when you feel rewarded each time you engage in a behavior.
- Focusing only on results keeps you from achieving results by distracting you from the process. Focusing on the process ensures you both get the results and enjoy the journey along the way.

Action Steps

1. Ask yourself, "What's my lesson from this?"
2. Considering the key areas of life that you'd like to improve, answer the following questions, being as brutally honest as possible.

- "If my habits stay the same as they are now, what will my life look like in a year? In five years? How painful would that feel?"
- "If I incorporated one breakthrough healthy habit into my life, how will my life be better in a year? In five years? How good will I feel?"

Day 2: The Seed of Transformation

In high school, I ate fast food every single night, and while not overweight, I was totally out of shape. By college, however, I was a health and fitness nut who you couldn't pay to touch junk food. I bench pressed twice my body weight, and I would never miss a workout if I could help it.

Did my habits from high school change by the time I got into college? Yes, of course. The real question though is, *why* did my habits change?

There was something that shifted *before* my habits, and it wasn't from a fairy sprinkling me with magic motivation dust, where suddenly out of the blue I felt like doing things I had despised just a few months earlier.

The first thing that changed was my *identity*. Another way of putting it is that my self-image of who I thought of myself as had changed, and as a natural consequence, so did many of my habits.

How did this happen?

First of all it took a belief that I *could* change. This is what comes from a growth mindset. I talk about the growth mindset early on because changing your identity is likely impossible from a fixed mindset. I was fortunate enough, probably because of how I was raised, to believe I could consciously choose to be the type of person I wanted to be. If you don't have a belief at this point that you can change your identity or grow significantly, don't worry. I'll share some strategies later in the book that will help you make this shift.

I will also point out that changing yourself doesn't mean changing who you fundamentally are. You don't have to pretend to be someone you're not. I'm referring to becoming your "best-self." As an analogy, an apple tree can never change nor should it try to change to become an oak tree, but it can still grow and change throughout the years to be a more developed apple tree that produces more fruit.

With my fitness transformation, I started reading information on the health consequences of the food I was eating. Before then, "unhealthy" was an abstract concept. I wasn't overweight, so why should I change how I eat? Once I realized that I was doing damage to my body, I had to ask myself, "Am I someone who has so little self-respect that I'll do this to myself, or am I someone who wants to take care of their body and be in great shape?" I *chose* to be a person who values their health, and my habits fell in line *after* that. I also saw myself as a "smart person." When I saw that my choices weren't smart, this conflict with my identity made me want to change my actions.

Another example is back when I was 12 years old and was getting into playing guitar. I remember going into a pawn shop and looking at guitars with my mom. The guy at the store said something along the lines of, "Get a cheap guitar because most people quit within a few months" while I was standing right there. While I appreciate the truth behind what he was saying, I took it as a slight insult. Just because most people quit after a few months didn't mean that *I* was going to quit. My best friend also told me I didn't have the discipline to play guitar because it was too difficult. His remark infuriated me.

When people told me I didn't have what it takes, I made a commitment to myself. I thought something like, "Damnit! I'm a person who can and will stick with what I say I'm going to do. I'll show these people! I'm going to be a badass guitar player." Fast forward ten years, and I was well on my way to getting my Bachelor's degree in music and guitar.

What's funny is, I'm not quite sure if I actually had the discipline to stick with it prior to it being implied that I might not. Before 12 years old, I can't think of anything I was particularly dedicated to. What I do know is that the anger I felt prompted me to commit to myself to prove to them and, most importantly, to myself, that I *did* have the discipline. I took on, *by choice*, the identity of someone who works hard and practices to become great at what they put their mind to.

This process also works in both directions, as you'll find out. Changing my behaviors also helped change my identity. You can start with either working on your identity *or* working on your behavior, and both will typically shift *together*. For now, however, let's work from the inside out to create a new identity for yourself so that your habits become almost an effortless extension of your personality rather than something that feels forced.

Recap

- You will do what's congruent with your identity, also known as self-image. Likewise, you will avoid doing what you feel is counter to your identity.
- You can change your identity with conscious intent.
- The process can also work in reverse. That is, changing your behaviors can change your identity.

Action Steps

1. Ask yourself, "What's my lesson from this?"
2. In what ways have you changed and evolved over the years?
3. If you were to meet the version of yourself that has reached their full potential, what kind of habits would they have developed?
4. Write down "I am committed to reaching my potential because…" and insert why this is so important to you.

Day 3: How Your Habits Work

Today you're going to get a basic overview of how the habit process works. You can use this knowledge to reprogram your habits using intelligent tactics that work *with* your psychology rather than *against* it. You'll also discover why bad habits are nearly impossible to break unless you do one thing *before* trying to break a habit.

Charles Duhigg lays out the three parts of the habit cycle in the book The Power of Habit. These three parts are:

1. The cue – What triggers the habit.
2. The routine – The habitual behavior.
3. The reward – The pleasure you get that makes you want to repeat the habit.

For instance, a person with the habit of nail biting when nervous may follow this cycle:

1. Cue – Feeling of nervousness
2. Routine – Nail biting
3. Reward – Feel calmer

A person with a habit of meditating each morning after coffee may follow this cycle:

1. Cue – Finish coffee
2. Routine – Meditate
3. Reward – Feel more focused and ready to take on the day

It's important to note that a variety of people can have the same habitual behavior, but get different rewards from it. For one person, they may eat ice cream each night as a way to feel pleasure after a stressful day. Another person may be using ice cream as a way of coping with feelings of loneliness. Still another person may use ice cream as a means to gain weight because they feel too skinny. The same behavior can have different emotional impacts for different people.

The reward is particularly important because without it, habits wouldn't form. The reward could be everything from pleasurable feelings of a dessert hitting your taste buds to the sense of accomplishment after an intense workout. Every behavior you engage in by free will choice, even the most destructive, provides some sort of emotional reward – or at least it did when you started to form the habit. Some habits no longer provide the reward they initially did, but they are continued because they have become a programmed pattern. In fact, the more something becomes a habit, the fewer emotions you feel when doing it.

The reason we feel rewarded by something emotionally is because it meets one or more of the six human needs. Cloe Madanes and Tony Robbins have talked about the six human needs that drive all of our behavior. Those needs are certainty (also referred to as comfort), variety (also referred to as excitement or entertainment), connection, significance, growth, and contribution.

The reason why it's hard for people to give up their old habits is because those habits meet one or more of those six human needs. If the only way a person feels significant is by cutting other people down, then they'll continue that behavior unless they can find another way to meet that need – hopefully a healthier way.

If a person does manage to give up an unhealthy habit but hasn't found a suitable alternative, they may simply trade one bad habit for another. Some people quit smoking only to develop a binge-eating habit.

Some finally get out of a bad relationship only to jump into another. Oftentimes we're not addicted to a behavior, we're addicted to the *feeling* a behavior gives us.

While this book will focus primarily on adopting healthy habits rather than breaking a bad habit, once you understand the emotional reward a bad habit is providing you, you can find a healthy habit to meet the same need(s). What happens then is that you may naturally drop the bad habit for a healthy habit *because you're getting the same emotional reward without the downside.*

This brings us to the final point – you don't truly get rid of bad habits. What you do is *substitute* a different habit to take its place. The wiring of a habit will always remain in your brain. What you'll be doing is training yourself to choose a better alternative so that eventually, your brain prefers the new pattern over the old.

Recap
- There are three parts to the habit process. 1) Cue 2) Routine 3) Reward
- Rewards are usually emotional. We feel a reward when we meet one or more of the six human needs.
- The six human needs are comfort, variety, connection, significance, growth, and contribution.
- Habits stay programmed in the brain. The way to overcome a bad habit is to find a better alternative or alternatives that meet the same emotional needs.

Action Steps
1. Ask yourself, "What's my lesson from this?"
2. Think of a habit you have, good or bad, and answer the following: What is my cue or reminder for the habit? *Is it something you just did, a place you're at, a feeling, person, or time of day?*
3. "What is the reward I get? *Is it a feeling of comfort and stress relief, excitement and fun, love and connection, significance, contribution, and/or growth?"*

Day 4: What Will Upgrade Your Life?

Your next step in the habit improvement process is to get clear on what habit upgrade you want to develop in your life at *this* moment. There's a good chance you already know what will help you move forward. If you're looking for ideas, the "5 Absurdly Simple Habits That Will Change Your Life" section, included as part of a bonus for this book, will help.

If you're primarily concerned with a bad habit you'd like to break, there are two things to consider. The first is that if it's a serious addiction, please seek professional help, because even if some of these practices will be helpful, this is not a guide meant for breaking addictions. The second thing to remember is, as you learned yesterday, you don't get rid of bad habits but you replace them with something better.

If you consider which of your human needs a bad habit is meeting, ask yourself, "Is there something better that will fulfill that same need or needs?" A person who is in the habit of watching TV for three hours every night may be looking for certainty/comfort. Another behavior such as getting a massage, meditating, or even exercising may be a better alternative for at least a portion of those three hours. A person who watches TV for three hours every night primarily for variety/excitement may choose to read a book, play a game with friends or family, or learn to play a musical instrument as an alternative.

For many people, their habits will be meeting *multiple* needs such as comfort, excitement, and connection all at once. One would need to consider an alternative or alternatives to satisfy all the needs their prior habit was meeting. This is especially helpful if someone simply wants to reduce the amount of time spent on a habit such as reducing three hours of TV watching down to one hour.

This can require some deeper understanding and awareness of how a habit is fulfilling you. This may take time, and it's *not* necessary to begin the habit change process. As you practice the exercises in this book and gain a deeper understanding of your unique psychology, over time you'll get a better idea of what drives you. Eventually, you'll be able to choose healthy habits that meet your needs.

The good news is there's something called "Keystone Habits" that seem to create a chain-reaction of positive change across many areas of life. For instance, when a person starts exercising, they may naturally want to start eating better. When a person starts practicing meditation, they may be more patient, focused, and proactive rather than reactive in what they do. When a person starts expressing gratitude to people on a regular basis, they may naturally start looking for other ways to improve their relationships since they'll be feeling a deeper sense of love and connection.

Here is a list of some common habits that can have a big carryover in all areas of life. I'll start with the bad habits, and then provide a suitable healthy habit which can be adopted.

Less Ideal Habits
- Poor diet
- Lack of exercise
- Withholding too much (communication, affection, attention, appreciation) from loved ones
- Not proactively managing one's emotional state and happiness
- Procrastination on important tasks
- Excessive distractions such as television, social media, and Keeping Up With The Kardashians

- Emotional outbursts later regretted
- Hanging around excessively negative people
- Complaining
- Not checking one's self-talk by saying things like "I suck" or "I'm not good enough" without questioning it

Healthy habits
- Nutritious diet
- Adequate exercise
- Openness with loved ones
- Managing one's emotional state
- Prioritizing important tasks and completing them before less important tasks
- Limiting entertainment to either after more important tasks are completed or during scheduled breaks
- Practicing mindfulness and using emotions to gain awareness
- Hanging around uplifting people who have what you desire
- Taking 100% personal responsibility
- Being mindful of self-talk and choosing to accept or reject it

You'll notice this list is full of broad concepts and has fewer specific action steps to implement. This is because, for instance, something like exercise has many different forms, and there's no one-size-fits-all recommendation. Your journey is to figure out what is ideal for you. Later in this book, you'll find out what I consider to be the best way ever to get a guaranteed game plan to hit your target goals.

Please also keep in mind that while I'm giving examples of poor habits, the goal of this book is strictly for developing healthy habits. Seeing examples of habits that are poor is simply meant to inspire you to think of better alternatives. With this challenge, you'll choose a *good* habit you want to adopt.

Recap

- Keystone habits create positive change in other habits.
- Focus on developing healthy habits which meet your needs.
- If you have a bad habit you'd like to break, seek specialized assistance with that. For now, realize developing better habits can potentially reduce your attachment to bad habits.

Action Steps

1. Ask yourself, "What's my lesson from this?"
2. Pick a healthy habit you'd like to adopt or improve upon that you feel will help you move forward in your life. At this point it's OK to be more general than specific. *Examples: Improve my diet. Show more appreciation. Meditate every day.*
3. Write down the healthy habit you're adopting in your daily action book.

Creativity Unleashing Questions

If you have trouble, use the creativity-unleashing questions below.

- "If there was one thing I'm doing holding me back from what I want, what would it be? What are some healthier alternatives that would fulfill me in the same way?"
- "If I knew one thing that would move me forward towards my goals in life, what would it be? If there was something else, what would it be?" *Keep asking and uncovering things.*
- "What's one thing I can start to implement *right now* to be even better?"

Day 5: Why You Don't Need Much Motivation to Succeed

At this point, you've identified a healthy habit that you want to incorporate in your life. It could be starting an exercise program, eating healthier foods, meditating, being more productive, reading more, or whatever else you feel will move your life forward.

Some people get to this point, and if they have a big change they want to make, they'll freeze up because it feels overwhelming. Since I'm a fitness coach, I'll use exercise as an example. Some of the challenges I hear people face when they want to start an exercise routine can include; getting new workout clothes, signing up for a gym or setting up a home gym, hiring a personal trainer or spending hours researching the right workout program, and/or overcoming feelings of being intimidated by others at the gym.

Even something as simple as getting into the habit of cleaning the house on a regular basis can feel overwhelming if someone doesn't know where to begin. When things feel overwhelming, it's helpful to remember a couple things. The first is the old question of, "How do you eat an elephant?" The answer is, of course - *one bite at a time*. Another thing I've heard from Alex Mandossian is that you can't do everything, but you can do anything *one thing at a time*.

What I've found is that more often than not, we usually know at least *one* way to move forward towards a goal even if we don't see the entire path to get there. Many years ago, before I figured out a great workout program to do in the gym, I started doing pushups and workout DVDs I found around my parents' house. I did *something* to start the habit of exercise and figured out the key details later. I also didn't know what the healthiest diet looked like, but I knew the sugary soft drinks and french fries weren't helping, so I cut those out.

I didn't make a complete overhaul of my lifestyle at first. Instead, I found a few simple tweaks that I didn't need to be a genius to know would help me get results that were at least a little better. Over time, I gradually built upon those habits through study and research to find even more effective ways to improve my health and fitness.

For the purpose of this book, realize that getting a perfect plan (which will never happen) isn't necessary. The key is to find a step that will move you in the right direction and then improve as you go. Getting a routine is the most important thing right now.

That means you want to start with a really small action you can do *every single day*. When I wanted to develop the habit of meditation, I set a target of 30 seconds of meditation each day. I knew that I could follow through with this *without fail* every day no matter how crazy that day was. In fact, it was so easy it would almost hurt my pride *not* to do it.

I could always do more if I wanted, and often I would once I got started. The key is that it was something I knew I would be able to follow through with consistently. Doing one push-up a day can eventually turn into an entire exercise routine over the course of a year. Giving one genuine compliment a day can turn into dramatically improved relationships and communication over the course of a year. The small steps make a big difference over time.

If you're familiar with the concept of "Tiny Habits" from BJ Fogg or "Mini Habits" from Stephen Guise of Deep Existence, you'll recognize this idea of choosing an extremely small target to hit each day in order to develop a habit. I'm going to refer to this concept as a "micro-habit." While it's great to pick something that is a bit of a challenge, given the choice between doing something you'll follow through with consistently vs. something you'll do sporadically, for the time being, consistency is the most important thing.

You may be wondering, "Why would something so small be worthwhile? I would never see results from doing a single push-up or thirty seconds of meditation!"

First of all, consider this. Have you ever started a task you didn't feel like doing at first, but then continued on effortlessly once you got into the swing of things? If so, you'll recognize a key concept that this entire approach is built upon: **Momentum creates motivation.**

Rather than trying to get yourself motivated before starting something, pick something so easy that you have no trouble getting started so that you create momentum – then the motivation will naturally follow. It may take a few days, weeks, or months to get into the groove, but eventually you'll find things become almost effortless.

If you want a big tree in your backyard, it's going to be pretty challenging to lift one out of the ground and stick it there. An easier approach is to start with planting a small seed and nourish it so it *naturally* grows to be a big tree. These tiny steps are the seeds to much bigger and better habits.

"Get obsessed with consistency." - Amir Siddiqui

Recap
- At first, consistency trumps all else.
- You often won't feel motivated until after you get started. Momentum creates motivation.
- The way to get started is to pick a tiny action so small and easy that it's almost effortless to do it each day. We'll call this your "micro-habit" upon which you'll build.
- The goal right now is developing a routine from which you will build upon. It doesn't matter whether what you choose produces results as long as it's a seed to a consistent process.

Action Steps

1. You will choose your micro-habit that you will engage in for the remainder of this book. This is a bare minimum action you will do every single day. It should take no more than five minutes, and ideally will be less than two minutes. You can always do more if you choose, however, realize it's not required to be "successful." *Tip: Choose something you're more likely to enjoy that still instills the positive habit. Hate exercising on the treadmill but love dancing? Start with dancing as a stepping-stone to other forms exercise. Prefer a guided meditation audio over doing it yourself? Start with guided meditation to make it easy on yourself.*

2. Write down your micro-habit in the form of "I am developing the habit of XYZ. My next daily step for this month is to... **insert micro-habit**"

3. Use your action guide to check off each day that you've completed your micro-habit. You can alternatively use a calendar system to create checkmarks. Tip: Some people like using Post-it notes they remove from a calendar (rather than creating a check) to see their successes each day.

4. Optional: Make it a game by tracking more data in your action guide. For example, with a reading habit, data can include time spent reading or number of pages read. Data with exercise can include sets, reps, and rest periods. Data gives you a means to track progress which can be helpful maintaining motivation.

Examples:

- "I am developing the habit of walking for exercise each day. My next daily step for this month is to walk to the end of the driveway and come back inside each day."

- "I am developing the habit of eating a healthier diet. My next daily step for this month is to take a couple minutes to make a smoothie in the morning."

- "I am developing the habit of being even more productive. My next daily step for this month is to schedule two minutes at the start of the day to work on important projects."

* Reminder: You can always do more than this. You may find two minutes turns into twenty minutes, and that's fine. Just don't *require* twenty minutes. A person who wants to get in the habit of going to the gym every day after work may say, "Just driving there will take more than five minutes so it's not a micro-habit." Realize that the micro-habit in that situation may just be changing into workout clothes after work, and that's *all* that's required each day. Going to the gym after changing clothes would be optional. If you find you can't follow through every single day with what you came up with, break it down into something even smaller. Can't make a smoothie each morning? Take out the blender, plug it in, and then put it back away for the time being. *The routine is more important at first than the results. You can always add more to the routine later!*

Bonus: In the back of this book, you'll find a kick-ass analysis of 5 reasons people fail at their mini-habits from Stephen Guise. Check it out!

Day 6: Remembering Your Habit

Congratulations! You have your habit picked out that you can do each day. You're probably feeling pretty good at this point because you know you'll be successful at doing this every single day for not only the remainder of this book, but you can easily do this far into the future. That's because your micro-habit is so quick and easy, you *can't* fail at doing it. Your goal right now is laying down a new pattern of behavior in the brain, and even the tiniest step in the right direction, when done every day, will solidify that process.

It's possible to end the book right here, and there's a chance you'd achieve some pretty remarkable results. You would create momentum with easy consistent actions which would get you motivated to do and achieve even more. However, there are still some potential pitfalls such as forgetting to do your new small habit, falling back into old routines after a stressful situation, and not knowing how to take it even further, to just name a few.

Let's tackle the first challenge, and that is remembering to do your new micro-habit. When I started a habit of doing ten seconds of handstands a day, I missed some days not because I didn't have the time or desire, but because I simply forgot about it. What I overlooked was not having a cue to signal me to do the habit. This also explains why if you've ever fallen out of a habit, say when going on vacation, it could be because the cue is no longer there.

The way I fixed that was by having a visual cue. I placed a piece of paper in my bedroom that said "10 second handstands." When I walked past the note to change my clothes, I would see it and do my handstands. Even if it was the end of the day when I would see the paper, I could still easily do ten seconds right before going to sleep. Micro-habits are great because they're so quick and easy that you can do them even if you're right about to crawl into bed.

A slightly more advanced tactic is to use one micro-habit to cue another habit. For instance, I can take a minute every day to put some fruits and veggies in a bowl that I set on my kitchen counter. This bowl then acts as a cue to remind me to juice them later in the day when I go back into my kitchen.

Another example of a visual cue would be if a person wants to get in the habit of flossing. Setting the floss right next to toothbrush so you can't miss it is the perfect visual cue. However, once you develop an association with brushing your teeth and then flossing, eventually the floss wouldn't always need to stay out and be visible.

As another example, when wanting to remind myself to eat more slowly, I set a reminder on my phone that constantly went off saying "eat slowly." I made it purposely go off every hour to be almost slightly annoying. While I'd still occasionally forget to eat more slowly, the key thing is I'd remember far more often. I'd also be mindful when eating, saying "eat slowly" to retrain my brain.

Besides sensory reminders like visual or aural cues, an easy way to cue a new habit is to tie it into something you already do every single day. I call this approach "This then that."

If a person wants to read a page of a book every day, they could set the cue as hitting brew on their coffee machine, reading that page while it brews, then drink their coffee. You're tying a new habit into an existing behavior.

Some other "this then that" approaches include:

- A commercial comes on, then do five pushups.
- Step out of the shower, then think of one thing to be grateful for.
- Put the toothbrush away after brushing at night, then get ingredients prepared for the next day's breakfast.
- Get in car after work, then drive to gym.
- Finish an assignment, then practice instrument for two minutes.

Finally, you can simply schedule a time of day to do the habit. I still suggest using a cue like an alarm going off to remind you to do it.

As to which type of cue is best, the answer is it depends. A "this then that" or scheduled approach is great if you have a very established routine each day that you can simply build upon. For myself, my schedule changes frequently, and I usually require more flexibility. Therefore I prefer something like setting a visual reminder that I know I'll see at *some* point everyday even if it's not the same time each day. Your micro-habit will be so small and easy that you can experiment to find what helps you the most without worrying about getting it wrong.

Note: A cue for a habit can also be an emotion, a person, a place, a scent, or other triggers. These can be a bit unpredictable and are not recommended at first for cuing a healthy habit.

Recap
- You need a cue to trigger your new habit.
- Your cue can either be 1) a visual or auditory reminder 2) a prior action in your routine 3) a time of day.

Action Steps
1. Ask yourself, "What's my lesson from this?"
2. Determine a cue for your new habit choosing either a visual or auditory reminder, "this then that," or time of day. If you're doing something like "this then that," it's

still OK to add in another reminder at first like a note.

3. Write down your cue in your action book using one of the following templates:

Option 1 - Reminder: "I will remind myself to do my habit of… by *insert daily reminder*." Example: I will remind myself to think of one thing for which I'm grateful each day by posting a note on my bathroom mirror that says, "What am I grateful for today?"

If you're creating a reminder such as a phone alert or written note, do that right now.

Option 2 - This then that: "After I do a *pre-existing routine*, I will do my new habit of…" Example: After I brush my teeth, I will meditate for thirty seconds.

Option 3 - Schedule: "At ABC time, I will do my new habit of…." Example: At 10:00am, I will do my new habit of doing at least ten push-ups a day.

If you're creating a reminder such as an alarm to go off at that time, set that up right now.

Day 7: The Right and Wrong Types of Rewards

Having a wedding coming up might be sufficient motivation for someone to lose twenty pounds in three months, but if their reward is simply getting to look good for their wedding day, what are the odds they're going to stick with their healthier behaviors after their wedding? Have you ever seen anyone hit a big goal only to indulge and slack off after they've hit their target?

This approach isn't ideal for developing long-term habits, at least not by itself. Long-term goals and corresponding rewards have their place. However, for a new habit to develop, you need a reward *every* time you do it. In other words, the delayed gratification typically associated with healthier behaviors is also what makes them so much more challenging to develop as habits when compared to guilty indulgences.

Luckily, you can create instant gratification *on-demand* when you understand a few things.

It's important to know the difference between intrinsic and extrinsic motivation. Extrinsic motivation includes external rewards like prizes and money. They can be helpful in some situations, but with habit development, we want to focus primarily on intrinsic motivation. With intrinsic motivation, the motivation or reward comes from within yourself. It's a positive feeling, a sense of accomplishment. When you enjoy a process for its own sake and do something "just for the fun of it," this is intrinsic motivation.

For people who get obsessed with a hobby that has no tangible payoff, such as playing music without getting paid for it, that is because they find it intrinsically rewarding. It's also feeling congruent with your values and identity as a person. If I see myself as a smart person, I would feel worse doing something I felt was stupid compared to making the "smart" choice, even if the stupid thing was more fun.

I hated the idea of exercise when I was younger. Why would anyone want to put themselves through pain like that? Now, however, I'll *gladly* put myself through pain for one big reason, and it's not because I want to look better, impress the ladies, or some other external factor (which are admittedly nice side bonuses). It's because I uncovered one thing that motivates me intrinsically – a challenge to beat my prior best and feel a sense of achievement.

When I got into weightlifting ten years ago, the feeling I got lifting a little more weight than the previous week gave me a sense of accomplishment that made exercise enjoyable. While I hate running for the hell of it, I'll gladly push myself to see if I can go a little faster than my previous best. It's not "fun" in a traditional sense, but it still has a certain intrinsic reward. Even if I don't beat a personal record, I can still enjoy seeing how far I can push myself. I get to say to myself, "Wow, Derek, you really kicked some ass today. How'd you get to be so awesome?"

This feeling of accomplishment, which arguably may be more commonly chased by men than women, explains the appeal of games. Rarely is anything gained of real value by playing games. It's simply the feeling that, "you accomplished something that took some effort" (combined with other factors) that creates a positive feeling that motivates the gamer to continue. As this book progresses, you'll learn other factors that motivate gamers and see how you can apply that information to motivating you to develop habits.

While it's good to know that finding something intrinsically rewarding will help you feel good every time you do it, what if you don't feel rewarded by doing something?

The first thing to understand is that if you have a particular story around something, like "reading is boring" or "I hate healthy food," it will be hard to turn those things into habits. Luckily, the solution is to reframe these things or simply change your focus. "What can I appreciate about reading? What do I love about healthy foods?"

Even with going to work, I would make it enjoyable by turning it into an opportunity to practice my social skills. I didn't just think of it as going to work, I thought of it as going to practice critical skills that were going to have a huge payoff in my life. If I were dealing with a customer who was a pain in the ass, my mental frame was "Great! I get to practice being more Zen in the face of adversity."

Another way to make something intrinsically rewarding is so simple that many people completely overlook it. I noticed when I would do this one simple thing, I would be able to change my emotional state around any activity *on demand*. I could literally feel good about almost anything if I did this enough.

That one thing I did was simply give myself positive self-talk after completing something. It could range from, "Good job!" to "Hell yeah!" to "Damn, Derek, you're the man!" The words, if any are used at all, don't matter. The point is I would simply take a moment after doing something to *allow myself* to take in the pride and satisfaction of being someone who follows through on what I set out to do – a core part of the identity I've chosen for myself.

It's this intrinsic type of immediate gratification after doing your new habit that you want to cultivate so that you enjoy that hit of pleasure every single time you do your habit. Don't worry if it doesn't come naturally at first. For those who aren't used to talking to themselves in a positive way, this will take some practice. Today's action step will help cultivate this.

On the flip side, this also means checking one's negative self-talk, which I definitely have fallen victim to at times. There are plenty of times where even though I did what I set out to do, I said, "Whatever... I should have done a lot more. It's sad that this is all I could do." If saying that is how a person "rewards" themselves for following through on their new habit, what are the odds it will stick? This negative self-talk is what sabotages people when they let it go unchecked.

Recap
- Delayed gratification doesn't work well for habit development.
- You can create immediate gratification when you tap into your intrinsic motivation.
- A simple way to do this is using positive self-talk and self-recognition.

Action Steps
1. Ask yourself, "What's my lesson from this?"
2. You can frame your habit by asking, "How could I see this as a game, a chance to help others, an opportunity to grow, a way to feel more secure, a time to feel more significant, or a chance to connect with others?"
3. Track your successes to feel a sense of accomplishment by checking off every day you complete your healthy habit on a calendar or in your daily action guide.
4. *Every* time after completing your micro-habit, take a few seconds to appreciate how you're becoming a better person. Congratulate yourself on a job well done. Ask yourself, "Why am I happy I did this? Why do I appreciate and admire myself for this?

Note: This doesn't need to take more than a few seconds. What it may take is practice to cultivate a good feeling if you're not used to it. If there are serious self-esteem challenges, then this can require some additional work. The good news is that this becomes a new, secondary habit tied to your first. *Rewarding yourself with positive feelings for a job well done is one of the best foundational habits you can cultivate to help you make progress in all areas of life.*

Day 8: Guaranteed Long-Term Success

Congratulations! You've made it through the first week. You should be doing your micro-habit each day after being prompted by your cue and rewarding yourself with self-praise, being sure to really enjoy the good feelings. Pretty simple process, right? Everything is in place for you to follow through perfectly and nothing could possibly go wrong.

Just kidding. Of course something can and likely will go wrong. The world and you aren't perfect. So while it's not good to assume you can't follow through each day, it's helpful to realize there are going to be the occasional slip-ups along the way. With that in mind, remember this:

A slip-up can either be good or bad depending on how you respond to it.

In the health field, I often hear stories about people who slip-up on their eating habits and say to themselves, "I ate really crappy these past couple days, so I might as well just indulge through the weekend and start fresh next week." With exercise I hear things like, "I missed exercising a few days, so I'll just forget about it this week and start over again on Monday."

If you missed a shower one day, would you wait until next week to start taking showers again? (Hopefully) Hell no! You'd go take a shower as soon as you got a chance. Why then would it be any different with any other healthy habit you're working to develop?

The reason why a person may be tempted to let a slip-up derail them is because of one key thing to understand. If momentum increases motivation, then a slip-up reduces momentum and, therefore, reduces your motivation.

Since a slip-up is likely to happen sooner or later, what do you do about it?

The answer is simple... *get back on track fast!*

As soon as you get a chance to do your micro-habit, do it. There's no need to get overly emotional about it. You don't need to have a breakdown because you forgot to floss one night. The unnecessary emotional rollercoaster some people put themselves through makes developing healthy habits go from a lot of fun to draining. Save yourself the trouble by saying, "This won't matter in the long-run *so long as* I get back into the swing of things **right now**."

It's important not to fall into the trap of overcompensation. For example, if someone missed their 30 minute workout one day, they could feel obligated to do a 60 minute workout the following day. This is a recipe for burnout. This is avoided altogether by only making your *micro-habit* a requirement. That means getting back on track should only take a couple minutes at most.

The second thing to do is ask yourself, "What can I learn from this?"

As I mentioned earlier, I missed some handstands when I was developing that habit. I learned I needed a better system to remind myself to do them. So I created one, and it was no longer an issue. In college, there were days where I wanted to work out in the school's gym, but I forgot my gym clothes that day. I learned to keep a change of clothes in my car at all times, so it wouldn't be an issue again. There were also times in college when I was on campus later than expected and only had fast food as a meal option. I learned to keep healthier snacks with me in case I was going to be out later than usual.

Even better than fixing slip-ups is to anticipate them ahead of time and be prepared. Consider what could possibly go wrong with your new habit and work out a contingency plan now to prevent it from becoming an issue. Also, mentally prepare yourself for how you're going to get back on track if/when a slip-up does occur.

Recap

- Slip-ups are your best opportunity to learn how to make your habits life-proof.
- When a slip-up occurs, get back on track fast and ask, "What can I learn from this?"
- Anticipate potential problems ahead of time and prepare for them right *now*.

Action Steps

1. Ask yourself, "What's my lesson from this?"
2. Write down the most likely challenges that will keep you from engaging in your new habit and what ways you can prevent them from ever being an issue. Implement these preventive measures immediately.
3. Reflect on how you will get yourself to get back on track should a slip-up occur.

Remember, right now you're only dealing with a very tiny new habit, something like reading a page of a book a day or walking for one minute. This means the challenges will also be small at this point. The most important thing right now is to adopt the mind-frame that a slip-up is simply a learning opportunity to do even better down the road.

Day 9: It's Your Life, Do What You Want

The beauty of the approach we're taking to developing healthy habits is that it relies on the smallest amount of willpower, rather than motivation, to get started. Like motivation, however, you may find your willpower is sometimes lacking a bit. What's been found is that the way we *perceive* something can affect our willpower.

Research has shown when people feel they're having to exert self-control out of obligation, such as to please others, it's more draining than those who exert self-control because they're following their own intrinsic desires. *Source: (Muraven)* In other words, if it feels like it's forced rather than a choice, it will be a lot more challenging.

In my experience, when I help someone out, say moving some furniture, because I see it as an opportunity to serve, it feels rewarding and good. If, however, I'm *commanded* to do something, say at a job where it feels like a chore, it becomes more mentally draining. The only real difference is how I'm mentally perceiving the situation. Is it something I feel I *must* do out of obligation, or is it something I feel like I *choose* to do out of free will?

Have you had the experience of finding something fun, then when you had to do it out of obligation such as part of a job, it lost its appeal? All that's happening is a change from "choose to do" to "have to do."

What does this have to do with habit development?

Consider this: Have you ever told yourself something like, "I can't have that chocolate cake. I have to get this work done. Stop watching TV, you lazy ass."

If so, you're using mental "boss" talk which creates resentment and feels like you're losing your sense of autonomy. It's natural to want to rebel against someone trying to take away free will, *even if that person is yourself!* This is called reactance.

If you're approaching your healthy habit as a command, and especially if you're replacing a bad habit with a healthy habit by telling yourself "I can't" do the old habit, you'll find yourself constantly struggling and draining your willpower. While this might not be a huge issue right now, it will make it difficult to grow your new habit into something even better.

How can you get around this?

It's a very simple two-part process. The first part is to use language that reflects that you're making a conscious choice rather than this being something you're forced to do – which ultimately is how it is anyway. We *always* have a choice and don't ever *have to* do anything. Even if a person puts a gun to your head, you can still choose not to do what they say, although it may not have the best of consequences.

Research has shown that when people used the restrictive word "I can't," they only made a healthier choice 39% of the time. However, those who said "I don't," which is more empowering because it represents making a choice, made a healthier choice 64% of the time. (Vanessa M. Patrick) Isn't it amazing the power that switching only one single word can have?

You can make an empowering shift by saying things like "I choose to," or other variations like "I want to," "I get to," and "I'm going to." For instance, "I choose to get three minutes of work done in the morning before anything else." "I'm going to meditate for at least a minute today." "I get to do some exercise this morning."

There's a second and very critical part to this process, and that's by adding in a compelling reason *why* you're engaged in the new habit. Your "why" is your motivator for action and will help you maintain perspective on the benefits of your new habit. You can do this by following up your statement with "because" and including the good reasons for doing the habit.

For instance, "I choose to make a smoothie this morning *because* it will make me feel energized, help keep me from getting sick, and get me the sexy body I've always wanted."

"I'm going to tell my partner one thing I appreciate about them today *because* I know it will make their day, make me feel all warm and fuzzy as well, and create an even deeper bond between us for a more fulfilling relationship."

Recap

- We often rebel against restrictions. This is called reactance.
- Bossing yourself around using language like "you must" and "you should" creates resentment and potentially drains willpower.
- Use language that reflects you're making a conscious choice because of the positive benefits.

Action Steps

1. Ask yourself, "What's my lesson from this?"
2. Create a compelling reason why you're engaged in your new habit with all the benefits.
3. Whenever you're going to engage in your new healthy habit, use *choice language* and reinforce your why by using a statement like, "I choose to do this because…."

Day 10: The Overlooked Key to Healthy habits

There seems to be one thing I've found consistently that separates those who are successful in sticking to their resolutions and those who give up. I'll give you a hint; it's the same reason why someone in the military will push themselves beyond their usual limits. It's the same reason a stay-at-home mom will make incredible sacrifices for her children. It's the same reason why a person will work tirelessly at a job they don't enjoy when they have bills to pay.

That one thing all of these people have in common is they're all held accountable. Accountability is often the missing link when it comes to making a change in your life because it provides something very helpful when first changing a behavior – avoiding pain.

Having to admit we've failed to follow through to someone is painful. It's even more painful if something else is on the line besides your pride, such as losing your job or letting down a loved one. This desire to avoid pain is a stronger motivator than the desire to gain pleasure.

How often will people *try* to make a change in their life but then not really put anything on the line? A New Year's resolution to stay in touch with old friends, start exercising, or get more sleep has no real painful consequence for not following through, at least in the short-term, unless you attach a consequence *yourself*.

Making a commitment to another person can potentially increase your likelihood of following through *if* you feel bad enough in telling them you didn't do what you said you were going to do. If telling a person you screwed-up isn't painful enough though, you can always add a punishment, or as I like to call it, a "motivator."

If I want to get a book finished, I can tell my friends I'll pay them $20 each if it's not done by a certain date. This keeps me accountable. As my friends will tell you, they've never yet gotten paid $20, although they're happy to check in with me when the date comes to see if my book is done. Giving up money is actually less of a motivator for me than my friends thinking I'm a slacker who doesn't do what he says he's going to do.

Common ways people stay accountable to others are with in-person meetup groups, classes and personal training, scheduling activities one must show up for, and online support groups. Having an accountability partner while going through the habit development process is highly recommended.

I've also had some success with self-accountability. Setting deadlines for myself and withholding pleasures if I don't follow through are some ways I can keep myself on track. This works only if you have enough self-discipline to hold yourself accountable for not following through.

While paying a friend money or cleaning their house as a consequence for failure makes a great motivator for bigger projects, what about the day-to-day habit stuff? I often use "motivators" like not letting myself watch TV until I've done the more important priorities for the day. For instance, no TV until after working out, meditating, or reading at least two pages of a book. This concept of saving something you enjoy until after doing something else works great for parents with their kids, and the good news is we don't change all that much in this regard when we grow up.

How you mentally frame this can be important. We don't want to create a negative association with the healthier behavior by saying something like "I can't watch TV until I do this stupid workout." You don't want the healthy habit to be the thing that's keeping you from what you enjoy, or a "necessary evil." Instead, the mental frame is, "If I want to watch TV later, *first I'll do something even better for me, like workout."*

The take-home point is that pain is a useful motivator, so use it well. Also remember that your punishments are ideally something that would benefit you anyway. That would either mean giving up something that's not moving you forward in life, like watching TV and surfing Facebook, or adding in something beneficial, like parking far away from your destination and walking a longer distance if you fail to follow through with your habit.

Recap

- Putting something on the line creates a pain avoidance motivation for a healthy habit.
- A punishment, also referred to as a "motivator," can help you stay on track.
- One type of motivator is to withhold a fun activity until you complete a habit.
- Another type of motivator is doing something beneficial although not particularly enjoyable like cleaning, walking further, or donating extra money to charity.

Action Steps

1. Ask yourself, "What's my lesson from this?"
2. Create a consequence for not following through with your healthy habit using one of these two formats:

- "If I want to do (enjoyable thing), first I'll do my more important habit of xyz." *Example: If I want to get on Facebook, first I'll do my more important habit of meditating for at least thirty seconds.*
- "If I don't do (habit), then I will (unenjoyable thing)." *If I don't meditate for at least 30 seconds every day this week, then I will clean my entire house and donate an extra $20 to charity.*

If you're doing everything right, it's unlikely you'll even need to use this because your daily habit is so easy. The key thing is having this in place so you remember that there is something on the line for not following through with what you commit to doing.

Highly Recommended: Find an accountability partner you can discuss this with. You can ensure that each person follows through with their commitments and punishments for any slip-ups.

Day 11: Using the Force Stronger than Willpower

One of the benefits of taking on a single small improvement is that it will require almost no willpower. There is one thing, however, that can be even stronger than willpower that you can use to skyrocket your results, or alternatively, will crush your potential if not managed properly. Eventually, this one thing will decide how far you can take your new habit, as well as how easy or difficult the journey will be. Wouldn't you like to make everything amazingly easy by tweaking one thing?

That one thing is your environment.

As Yogananda says, "Environment is stronger than willpower."

Let's say someone is working on the habit of healthier eating and they have a kitchen filled with junk food. Would it make more sense for her to constantly fight cravings to pig out each time she goes to the kitchen or to spend one day throwing out all of that stuff and replacing it with healthier food? If there are other people in the household, she could put the food into a different cabinet that she then refuses to look into.

If you have limited willpower, that willpower is best invested in setting up a positive environment rather than wasted on having to fight against a poor environment.

Keep in mind that while you can't always get rid of negative environmental influences such as co-workers and family members, you can usually always do something to add in more positive influences. Listening to books on tape and podcasts on occasion while driving rather than listening to music is a way that I managed to bring more positivity into my life.

Another thing to consider about your environment is task association. Some people associate their bedroom with sleeping and relaxation, so it doesn't make a good exercise environment for them. Some people may associate their office with work, so it doesn't make a good meditation environment for them.

This explains why a lot of people who work on a laptop may go to a coffee shop to get work done rather than do it at home. Remembering the habit process, this environment acts as a *cue*. Have you ever noticed that simply being in a particular environment triggers a mood for you? A change in environment can easily create a different state.

Some ways people may manage their environment include:

- Posting inspirational pictures and quotes where they can be readily seen.
- Getting rid of or hiding temptations such as unhealthy food.
- Shutting off or turning phones to airplane mode when doing important tasks.
- Using a program to block distracting websites during work hours.
- Spending more time around uplifting people and less time with poor influences.
- Posting a calendar with checkmarks for completed tasks and daily habits in a visible place to be reminded constantly of the progress being made.

Recap

- "Environment is stronger than willpower." – Yogananda
- Rather than using willpower to fight against a poor environment, use it to setup an environment that ensures success.
- Getting rid of negative influences isn't always practical nor always necessary. You can, however, almost always bring in more positive influences.
- Some environments aren't inherently good or bad, but may be more readily suited to certain tasks depending on how they affect your state.

Action Steps

1. Ask yourself, "What's my lesson from this?"
2. For the healthy habit you're developing, answer the following: "In what ways could my environment be holding me back? In what ways can I make my environment even better?"
3. After responding to those, pick the #1 way to improve your environment, and go implement it right now.

Note: While you might not be able to completely overhaul your environment, you can likely make it at least a *little* bit better. Ask yourself, "What's one tiny thing I can do to make my environment even better?"

Day 12: How You Can Feel Ridiculously Awesome On Command

It's time to let you in on one of several "hidden" lessons in this book. While you're learning about developing habits, you're actually learning some far more important lessons about human behavior and improving your life. One of these hidden lessons is that the internal affects the external *and* the external affects the internal.

What do I mean by that?

The typical model of behavior is that how we think and feel internally affects what we do externally. This is true. Changing your thoughts and feelings will typically change your actions. However, the reverse is also true. Your actions can determine how you think and feel.

With micro-habits, you don't have to *feel* like doing them. What you'll probably find, though, is that by taking action, your feelings start to shift. Eventually, you'll want to do even more good things for yourself.

This is important to know, because many times, you're not going to *feel like* doing the very thing that's going to help you make a breakthrough. You might even be feeling so down that you lack the creativity and drive to make anything happen other than sitting around with a tub of ice cream and watching the Bachelorette. In times in which your emotional state has crashed, do you want to be doomed to feeling like crap and not getting anything done, or would you like to know a simple way to keep moving forward?

Hopefully by now you know it's possible to take a proactive and practical approach. This proactive approach is referred to as "state management."

Using one type of state management technique, researchers were able to increase or decrease test subjects' testosterone and cortisol levels a statistically significant amount in a matter of minutes. This was without ingesting anything or doing any type of exercise.

The one simple thing they had these subjects do was change their body posture. A powerful posture, such as taking up more space or raising one's hands in the air in a V shape led to favorable hormone changes in both sexes. A timid posture led to unfavorable changes. *Source: (Dana R. Carney)*

Think about that for a moment. You can literally start altering your hormones and mood right now by changing the position you put your body into. Have you ever noticed that just putting a big goofy smile on your face can actually make you feel happier? What if all it takes to get motivated is to move your body differently? Pretty incredible, right?

Another example of something you can proactively do to manage your emotional state is to listen to music. As a musician, this is often my go-to method to uplift my mood. Yet, despite using music my whole life to change my mood, even I forget about it at times when I need it the most. I'll sit down to write or get work done and be thinking, "Ugh, I don't want to do this right now." However, I can turn on background Baroque music which, rather than being entertaining, is used to focus the mind and helps me get work done. Music then goes from being a form of recreation to being a practical tool to strategically alter my mood.

Knowing you can manage your state is only half the battle. *Remembering* to manage your state when it is poor is the real key to success.

Another form of state management that's rarely talked about is what you're wearing. I work from home so sometimes I wake up and then try to get to work in the same clothes I was sleeping in. What I find is that I'm not as effective as if I put on nicer clothes first. This is because of how I've task-associated the type of clothes I'm wearing to what I'm doing.

Want to get in the mood to exercise? Put on workout clothes, and see how you feel. Want to get in the mood to make things happen? Put on dressy business attire, and see how you feel. Want to get in the mood to unwind and meditate? Take *off* the business attire, and put on something more comfortable.

Just like you can create a certain environment such as a meditation space to cue a desired habit, you can use the clothes you wear to cue a desired state. With your new emotional state, engaging in the habit becomes easier. It's these surprisingly simple and sometimes overlooked things that can make a huge difference.

There are several other forms of state management which will be revealed later in this book. For now though, realize that simple changes in body posture and movement like dancing, the music you listen to, and the clothes you wear will help set the mood to do your healthy habit even more.

Recap
- Your motivation can go up or down depending on your emotional state.
- You can proactively manage your state rather than letting your state manage you.
- A few ways to alter your state are with physical movement, music, and the clothes you wear.

Action Steps
1. Ask yourself, "What's my lesson from this?"
2. Before *and* after doing your healthy habit, take a few seconds to create a positive state for yourself by combining your positive self-talk with some physical

movement like a fist pump, dancing, and/or putting a big smile on your face.

Example: After completing a healthy habit, I may say "Yes!!" while doing a fist pump and smiling. It's as ridiculous as it sounds, which is bonus points for making me laugh at myself when I do it. This reinforces a positive association with the healthy habit. I may also take a minute to turn on some upbeat music and dance to get myself in a better mood before engaging my healthy habit.

Day 13: What Crazy Sports Fans Can Teach You about Habits

At the start of this book, I talked about the first transformation that took place before my habits followed suit. That was the transformation of my identity. At this point, you may have started to take on a new identity as a response to regularly doing your healthy habit. For instance, if a person starts meditating each day, eventually, they'll start to think of themselves as a meditator. The only problem with this approach is that it can take a while.

What if there was a way to shortcut the process?

Fortunately, there are a couple tricks that can be used to make this process go even faster. It's not a replacement for some serious therapy if that's what a person needs, but it will get you moving forward in just a few moments a day.

Before I get into the techniques, I'm going to show you how you can almost psychically predict whether or not something is a habit for someone without them ever telling you how much they do it. It's by looking for signs in their language.

Who do you think is more likely to exercise as a habit, a person who says "I didn't get in my workout today" or "I didn't get in a workout today?" Did you catch it? How about this? Who's the regular coffee drinker, the person who says "I didn't have a cup of coffee this morning" or "I didn't have *my* morning coffee?"

The subtle difference between these phrases is the use of the word "my." If something is a part of your lifestyle and routine, you may occasionally use the word "my" in how you refer to it which indicates a closeness and connection.

People even say "my team won the game" when they're referring to a sports team they're cheering for. Logically of course, sitting on the couch rooting for a team doesn't make them "your" team in that you have no direct ownership and aren't on the team. Yet, this type of language reflects an *internal* connection that's been made to something. No wonder then that when some people create this type of mental and emotional connection they go cray cray and start riots when "their" team loses.

Another example of the type of language people use when they have an identity with something is a little more obvious, and that's using "I am" type of statements. When I first started playing guitar, I would say that "I'm a guitar player." The more I stated this, the more likely I would be to live up to my identity by playing more guitar. With health and fitness, I would state things like "I'm pretty health conscious" or even jokingly, "I'm a health nut," along with "I'm a weight lifter" even though I never competed.

When a coach referred to me as an "athlete," and a mentor referred to me as an "entrepreneur," I began to think of myself as those things. However, prior to getting those labels, I didn't see myself as those things. Have you ever tried to live up to a positive trait that's been put on you? If so, you know the power this can have.

While the words we use are a reflection of our internal beliefs, we can hack this process and go in *reverse*. *That means that changing your language can, potentially over time, change your beliefs and identity.*

If you've ever done affirmations, making statements like "I am a winner" or "I am irresistibly sexy," then you know about their use for upgrading your identity. You may also know they're not always that effective for a number of reasons. The first and foremost reason is that if your brain is telling you, "That's not true!" then it will have a hard time accepting it. That doesn't mean affirmations can't be useful, it just means we must be more *tactical* in how we use them.

I've found a way to make affirmations more effective is by doing one of two things. The first thing is to use affirmations that are believable. In music school, I didn't think of myself as a good lyricist, and to be honest, I'm probably not that great. However, that identity wouldn't help me when I had to write lyrics. So I picked something I did believe in – that I'm a good writer. I also believed that I was creative. Taking two existing identities I had, I was able to coax myself into starting to accept a third belief – that I could *become* a good lyricist because of my creativity and writing skills.

This meant making statements like, "I'm a great writer and creative, and I'm using those skills to become a better lyricist." If I were to make that statement today, I would say "become an *even better* lyricist." The phrase "even better" implies some degree of competency already and is a subtle way of building belief in yourself.

The second method is to use embedded statements such as asking a question like, "Why am I a health conscious person?" or "How am I becoming more of a great writer?" Both of these questions imply that being health conscious and being a great writer are *already* part of who I am. Naturally, you can apply this to take on whatever kind of identity would be most useful for you and the habits you'd like to develop.

Recap

- Changing your language can alter your identity and beliefs.
- Saying things like "my" when referring to your healthy habit creates a stronger connection.
- "I am" affirmations can be effective for reinforcing a new identity if the statement is believable. Alternatively, embedding statements into questions works as well.

Action Steps

1. Ask yourself, "What's my lesson from this?"

2. Come up with a word, usually ending in "er" or "or," that embodies someone who does your healthy habit. It should resonate with you, so feel free to even make up a word if it's helpful. *Examples: If the habit is to read each day, you'd be a "reader." If it's meditating, you'd be a "meditator." If it's to exercise, you'd be an "exerciser" or a "fitness enthusiast."*

3. Come up with a question and statement about your healthy habit using this format. "What do I enjoy about being a _____? I appreciate MY habit of _____ because _____" *Example: What do I enjoy about being a healthy eater? I appreciate **my** habit of eating healthy because I love taking care of my body, having tons of energy, and looking ridiculously amazing.*

4. Use the word "my" whenever you can refer to your healthy habit. If you're trying to distance yourself from a bad habit as well, avoid using the word "my" when referring to it.

Bonus: Mirror Technique

If you really want to supercharge the effect of affirmations, you can use a technique I've found very helpful. You look in the mirror and make convincing statements to yourself like "I am strong and courageous," or alternatively, "YOU are courageous." This helps reinforce a new identity. When done in a peak emotional state and with the full force of your emotions (as opposed to just going through the motions), you'd be surprised at how powerful this can be. This can be done on a "need to do" basis when feeling down and not as motivated.

Day 14: Escaping the Black Hole of Repeated Mistakes

Have you ever studied hard for a test in school, did well on the test, and then a week later you forgot almost everything? If someone reminded you of an answer, you may even respond with, "Oh yeah, I know that," but it would be next to impossible to remember it off the top of your head.

The next thing to consider is, have you ever read a book and learned a lot of cool tips and tricks, only to find when it comes time to actually remember that stuff in the real world when you need it most, the insights don't readily come to you?

I'm willing to bet there's a lot of concepts in this book that you're already familiar with. Yet what we usually need isn't learning something new, it's being *reminded* of what we already "know." I teach this stuff, and even I forget it on occasion. So isn't it fair to say that knowing something already doesn't really matter unless you remember it when you need it?

There's one thing I started doing, taught to me from my greatest mentor, which helped me *truly* learn and apply the important lessons I got each day. Doing this one thing kept me from repeating the same mistakes over and over. This one simple practice takes what you've learned and drives it down to your core so you carry it with you every day.

That one thing is having a nightly review of my day. I do this as I'm getting ready for bed, and it only takes a couple minutes. Yet, the simple act of reviewing the things that worked well and what I could do better helps ingrain the concepts in my brain.

A great coach will often ask you, "How did this help you?" and "What's something you can do even better?" along with other questions that force you to think. This act of analyzing and processing the information is what makes information stick over the long-haul.

Recap
- We often know what we need to do. What's critical is *remembering*.
- Reflecting on your experience of the day ensures that the lessons stick.

Action Steps
1. Ask yourself, "What's my lesson from this?"
2. Have these questions written or printed out and placed next to where you go to sleep as a cue to ask them before bed. Your answers can change a bit each day.
- "What did I find that helped me stick with my habit today?
- "What can I do even better?" (Especially important if you didn't do the habit.)
- "What do I enjoy about being a _____? I appreciate MY habit of _____ because _____."

Example:
1. *"I found that doing my exercise routine as soon as I get home from work (before I had a chance to sit down on the couch) kept me from getting too tired to get started."*

2. *"Tomorrow, I will keep my workout clothes in my car so I can go to the gym before even stopping by the house."*

3. *"I enjoy being an exerciser because I feel like a badass when I push my limits. I appreciate my habit of exercise because I have more energy, I like the way I'm starting to look, and I'm proud of knowing I can overcome challenges that used to hold me back."*

Day 15: Simpler Is Smarter – True or False?

It's now time to start the process of taking your habits even further. While up to this point we've been focusing more on the process rather than the results, naturally you want to get great results as well. If you're already getting great results, well then, you'll probably want to get even better results.

The thing about results is that they can be a great indicator of how effective your habits are. If a person has been exercising for an hour a day, six days a week, trying to lose weight, and nothing has budged for the last six months, it's a good indication that something needs to change. While it's great this person has a habit of exercise, it also becomes kind of silly if they aren't seeing the results they want with that habit *after a prolonged period of time*. Isn't it pretty obvious that if something isn't working that you need to do something different? The key, of course, wouldn't be to necessarily change the *fundamental habit* of exercise, but to tweak it a bit, such as changing the particular exercise routine up.

There's an important difference between starting something and improving something. When you first start, it's all about *subtraction*. Subtraction means ignoring all kinds of things to bring your mind focused on a single action or two that you can take. This focus prevents you from feeling overwhelmed – which is quite common when tackling something new. Micro-habits are the ultimate in simplification. A single act that takes less than a couple minutes. Pretty freakin' easy, right?

This is also why simple suggestions are given to people when they're stuck in "paralysis by analysis." A person who is overwhelmed by the process of losing weight may be told, "Just eat less, and move more." This can be a great recommendation for someone overthinking things, but it's a worthless thing to say to someone who is already very health conscious and struggling with their weight for other reasons. It's *too* simple and not necessarily accurate in certain contexts. Have you ever been frustrated because advice was too simple to be helpful for where you were at and didn't address key details? You can see that sometimes we need to add in particular details and caveats to "complicate" things a bit.

To use a non-fitness example, a person working on their relationship may be given the recommendation to "say something you appreciate about your partner each day." This is a great recommendation and makes for an awesome micro-habit. The problem is that it can become a thoughtless routine and, most important, is only *one of many* factors involved in having good relationships. The simplicity of the recommendation is great, so a person can start improving their relationships without getting overwhelmed by all the things they can work on. The simplicity is also the downfall if it's *all* a person ever does, because eventually the growth in the relationship will stop if it's based entirely on this one act.

Subtracting and simplifying gets you started. Adding and upgrading keeps you growing.

This is a back and forth process, and we're now ready to focus heavily on the "addition" or growth phase of your healthy habit development. In reality, we've been adding something each day. Yet, because it was only one or two new additions, it never felt overwhelming. This one-step-at-a-time process is how you grow. We're after this Yin Yang balance of keeping it simple enough that you can act on it, but adding in something new so you keep progressing.

To add without overwhelming, there are my "3 Magic Words" coming up later in this book that is hands down the most effortless way to do this that I've found. For now though, we'll need a bit of self-assessment for how to improve upon your current habit.

There are three ways to improve habits:

1. **Increase quantity.** Examples: Go from meditating 30 seconds a day to 2 minutes a day. Go from asking yourself what is one thing you're grateful for each morning to asking yourself what two things you're grateful for are.

2. **Change quality.** Examples: Go from walking to jogging. Go from checking in with one old friend a week through email to checking in with one old friend a week with a phone call.

3. **Add a new habit.** Examples: In addition to the habit of making a healthy lunch, add in the habit of making a healthier dinner. In addition to the habit of strength training, add in the habit of flexibility training.

Recap

- Simplifying things helps you get started and move forward.
- When things are kept too simple, it can stagnate progress. Addition or change is necessary for growth.
- New details should be added slowly, no more than a few things at a time, to prevent getting overwhelmed.

Action Step

1. Ask yourself, "What's my lesson from this?"
2. Come up with one way to make your healthy habit even better. Can you increase the quantity, change the quality, or add some other component to it altogether?
3. Ask, what is a challenging but *realistic* target to shoot for with my habit upgrade that can be accomplished most

days? Example: *"My micro-habit is reading for one minute a day, and I can realistically strive to read for ten minutes a day most days."*

Please note, the bare minimum micro-habit you've been doing each day is still *all* you need to do each day to be successful. The upgrade is something to strive for, which you may or may not hit each day. At no point, not even a year down the road, do you need to increase your micro-habit. Doing more is something you *allow* rather than *force*.

Practical Personal Story: In the process of writing this book, I was working on improving some habits of my own. One habit I'm developing as of writing this book is to make fresh fruit and vegetable juice once each day. My micro-habit is to simply set a bowl of fruits and veggies on the counter in my kitchen, typically when I'm making coffee in the morning. This also acts as a cue so when I go into the kitchen again later, I see the bowl and am reminded to make juice.

On a time-crunched morning, I was going to run out of the door without enough time to make juice. I would be gone all day and wouldn't likely want to make juice when I got back home late that night right before bed. Knowing this, I *still* set the bowl on the counter while making my morning coffee even though I knew I'd probably just put it back in the refrigerator. I do my micro-habit even if there seems to be no practical benefit because the real benefit early on is creating a consistency in my routine. Remember, many micro-habits by their very nature are so small that the benefits aren't from the direct results they create, but rather from the momentum they create.

Because I had been juicing each day for the past week, the power of momentum kicked in and spurred me to want to still do something beneficial. When I realized I wouldn't have time to juice, I grabbed a plastic Zip-Lock bag and stuck some celery and carrots in there from my bowl to have as a snack later in the day. While I didn't get in my juice, I still got in some vegetables I may not have otherwise eaten.

Why is this so significant?

I didn't lose sight of my *big picture* intention which is to keep my health strong by eating enough fruits and vegetables. While juicing was a specific way of accomplishing that, I didn't get so focused on that habit as being my *only* means to an end.

Another hypothetical example could be if a person is developing the habit of reading a chapter of a personal development book each day and they find themselves without their book, they could still get on a blog and read some personal development or download a podcast. Someone who usually workouts at a gym but can't make it one day could still do some bodyweight exercises just to keep up the habit of doing *some* daily exercise.

The power of some of the recommendations in this book may not seem relevant to you at first. Give it time though and you'll start to notice how these seemingly insignificant things lead to something much greater in the long-term.

Day 16: 3 Magic Words to Effortlessly Overcome Overwhelm

If I could give someone a single piece of advice to overcome overwhelm, start improving their habits, and explode their productivity, it would be teaching them how to use my "3 Magic Words."

These three magic words are also perfect for the occasional "I should do that" type of things that come up, but might not be made into a regular *daily* habit. For myself, that would be something like cleaning my apartment, which I often procrastinate doing. I don't necessarily need to get into a *daily* habit of cleaning my apartment, but I'm going to have some problems if I don't do it at least once every few weeks.

The three magic words technique is done by asking the question, "Can I just…?" and inserting an action so easy that I'm guaranteed to be able to do it even if I have barely any willpower at all.

Let's say I don't feel like doing an hour-long workout. I can ask, "Can I just do the warmup?" If even that's too overwhelming, I'll ask, "Can I just do the first 30 seconds?" After that I'd ask, "Can I just do a little more? One more rep? One more exercise?" I can always stop once I've reached a point where I've felt like I've done all I can and still feel a sense of accomplishment.

Have you ever noticed that, even if you dreaded doing something, it was a lot easier once you got started? This is the power of momentum. The key is to pick such an easy starting point that you can get that ball rolling.

Instead of trying to get motivation, try to get momentum. The motivation will naturally follow.

I can even add an escape clause to this by adding "and if I want to quit, I can," or "if I want to do something else, I can." Using the apartment cleaning example, I would ask myself, "Can I just wipe off the counter top and then I can quit if I want?" There's a good chance I'll just keep on going after that. I can ask, "Can I just put away the dishes and leave the rest for tomorrow if I want?" "Can I just eat a healthy salad for dinner and see if ten minutes later, I still want the dessert?" What often happens is just by knowing in the back of my mind that I can quit if I want, it removes the resistance to getting started.

Besides an escape clause, I can add a condition that takes pressure off myself to be perfect. "Can I just write one *really crappy* sentence in my next book and then I can always make it better later?" "Can I just do a few really sloppy pushups and then see if I feel like doing more?" "Can I just order the slightly less unhealthy meal option I see on the menu?"

What I'm doing is a couple of things. I'm picking something so small and easy that I can't say no, and I'm giving myself an out (I can quit and don't need to be perfect) so it doesn't feel forced. It's the same concept of a micro-habit, but now you can turn *anything* that comes up in your life into a too-easy-to-say-no-micro-action.

Overwhelm comes from seeing all the steps in the process at once. If I'm thinking about the 37 things I have to do to complete my next book, I'm naturally going to put it off. If I only ask, "Can I just do the next thing on my list?" such as naming the next chapter, it suddenly becomes far easier to get going. Best of all, once I get going, then I usually want to *keep* on going. This has also been the experience of many other people I've taught this technique to.

This technique can not only be used to get you started with something by simplifying it, but it also works to help you *upgrade* your current habits.

Let's say I set my target of doing thirty seconds of meditation for the day. Around thirty seconds I can ask myself, "Can I just do another thirty seconds?" It's so easy at that point that it's hard to say no. Boom! I've just doubled my habit effortlessly. I can then ask after that thirty seconds, "Can I just add in one more minute?" If at some point I do feel like quitting, I have two options; I can either try to do something even less like, "Can I just do ten more seconds and see how I feel?" or I can quit for the day.

It's better to shoot for one minute of activity and optionally turn it into ten minutes than to shoot for ten minutes and feel like a failure if you don't do it. Remember, so long as you hit your minimum target of your tiny habit, you're a success. Even if the answer is "no" for the day of doing just a little extra, remember that you succeeded as long as you did your micro-habit for the day.

One thing I want to address are two big ways I've seen people screw this up. The first way is by being too vague. "Can I just eat healthier?" is vague. "Can I just eat one piece of celery with my lunch?" is specific. "Can I just walk more?" is vague. "Can I just walk for thirty seconds to the end of my driveway and back?" is specific.

The other way people screw this up is that they choose an inaction. For instance, "Can I just *not* indulge on junk food on the weekends?" You want to use this with a specific action to strive for proactively. A better alternative might be, "Can I just order a salad and see if I still feel like eating any junk?" "Can I just drink a glass of water and eat a piece of fruit and see if I'm still craving a snack after ten minutes?"

Note, if someone still feels like indulging after ten minutes, that's OK. One can have their treat. For the time being, the priority is to be proactive about doing more healthy actions.

This method cannot fail so long as you break it down into something so easy that it requires virtually no effort and time. Even if it takes months to build momentum, using these three magic words, *"Can I just"* to find the smallest step you're willing to take, is guaranteed to take you farther than doing nothing at all.

Recap

- Instead of telling yourself to do something, *ask yourself* if you're willing to do it.
- Break the behavior you're striving to do down into the smallest first step that's so easy you can't say no.
- Ask yourself, "Can I just do this tiny step?" If the answer is no, break it down even more to something stupidly easy.

Action Steps

1. Ask yourself, "What's my lesson from this?"
2. Whenever you're done with your micro-habit, ask yourself "Can I just...?" and see if you're willing to incorporate one of the upgrades you picked yesterday in a gradual manner. *Examples: "Can I just read one more page in this book?" "Can I just meditate for another 30 seconds?"*
3. Optional – If there's something you often procrastinate with, use the "Can I just...?" method to pick the tiniest starting point and then you can quit. *Examples: If someone wanted to start writing a paper, they could ask, "Can I just open my word processor and write one sentence?" If someone wanted to start organizing their closet, they could ask, "Can I just open my closet and move just one thing I see in there?"*

Day 17: Why Sacrifice Doesn't Have To Suck

If someone offered me either a piece of chocolate cake or an apple and asked which I would rather have, my default reaction is going to be to take the piece of cake every time. I would want what's going to provide quickest reward of pleasant feelings.

Now let's switch things up a bit. Let's say someone showed me two potential futures twenty years down the road. The first is of me being out of shape, sick, and tired. The second is of me being in great shape, in radiant health, and full of energy. If they asked me which I would rather have, of course I'd take the second option.

The point is that we have conflicting desires. What we want in the short-term doesn't always align to the outcome we want in the long-term. Now there's nothing wrong with chocolate cake on occasion. The point isn't that you can't ever have treats. Rather, it's that if you want have your long-term desires, there's going to need to be, *on occasion,* a sacrifice of your short-term desires. Think about anything significant you've accomplished in your life. Did you have to sacrifice something else you would have enjoyed in the short-term to get it?

Since sacrifice is essential, let's first take a look at the word itself. Sacrifice sounds inherently unpleasant, but if you think about it, you're constantly making sacrifices. Every time you watch TV, you're sacrificing the opportunity to do anything else in the world at that moment besides watching TV. By picking one particular show to watch, you're sacrificing every other show or movie you could be watching. The same goes for everything else that you do. Every time you say "yes" to something, you're saying "no" to something else. The question becomes, "Is what I'm saying 'yes' to important enough to say 'no' to something else significant in my life?"

While this is common sense when you think about it, it's also an important reminder. You're *always* giving up something. Yet we hate to ever feel like we're "giving up" something we like, even if it's for a greater good. This struggle is how we can get so conflicted about all kinds of things. This is why I prefer to mentally reframe sacrifice or "giving up" as merely an *exchange,* or better yet, an "upgrade."

A good exchange will leave you with something better than what you traded it for. If I paid $1,000 for a bottle of water, I'd be pissed off and feel like I got screwed. That is, unless I was dying of thirst, in which case it would be a worthwhile exchange. I'd be giddy as a schoolgirl feeling like I got an awesome deal to exchange $1,000, or even my current car for that matter, for a Lamborghini. In all of these situations, I sacrifice $1,000, something I don't normally like to give up. However, my feelings about it differ radically depending on whether or not I feel it was a *worthwhile* exchange or an upgrade. In other words, do I walk away from the exchange and think, "That was totally worth it!"

If you haven't guessed it, we're now getting into a key roadblock that will keep you from taking your habits to the next level. That roadblock would be *whatever is holding you back that you must give up* to make even more progress.

For a person wanting to eat healthier foods, the roadblock could be junk or convenience food, or things that occupy their time keeping them from preparing better food. For a person wanting to be more productive, it could be distractions, such as social media. For a person wanting to get in better shape, it may even be a desire to do easy exercises rather than something more intense.

The problem is it's hard to give up something you enjoy doing by sheer willpower. As we've covered earlier, our natural reaction to someone telling us to give up a pleasure is to fight against it. It's the whole "don't tell me how to live my life" reaction called reactance.

Luckily, we can combine two things to get around this. The first is to do like we did before, and turn a command into a choice by asking a question. The second thing is to give yourself more perspective on the *long-term* consequences of your options.

The question takes the form of "Would I rather?" where you present two options and, very importantly, provide the negative consequences of the behavior you want to avoid and the positive consequences of the healthier behavior you want to adopt. It's especially helpful to use emotional language including how you'd *feel* about each choice.

Let's say a person wants to exercise more but kicking back on the couch is looking very tempting. They could ask: "Would I rather watch TV and slow down my progress then end up feeling guilty, OR *can I just* do at least five minutes of exercise, feel great about myself, and keep my healthy exercise habit going to get that six pack I've always wanted?"

If someone wanted to get in the habit of being productive in the morning, but they're eager to check Facebook, they could ask, "Would I rather get on Facebook knowing I'll get sucked into it and an hour will pass by and I'll feel like a total lazy idiot for having wasted so much time, OR *can I just* spend at least 10 minutes working on my business plan so I feel amazing about myself, knowing I will be financially free so I can take the vacation I've always wanted?"

Did you notice how easily the "Can I just?" can be incorporated into this question?

It's also important to remember that if your answer occasionally is you'd rather do the less ideal thing, that's OK! Sometimes I'll eat the chocolate cake and watch TV. We're not after perfection and living a super boring life here. Instead, this question will help you make better and better choices each day progressively leading, over time, to even more incredible results in your life.

Recap

- You must sacrifice or exchange things at some point to make progress.
- Sacrifice only sucks if you focus on the short-term pain rather than long-term gain.
- To make a healthy decision, switch your perspective to the long-term consequences when thinking about that choice.

Action Steps

1. Ask yourself, "What's my lesson from this?"
2. Consider the following: "What behavior(s) holds me back?" or "How am I holding back from my potential?"
3. Think of a "Would I rather?" question that incorporates the consequences of various choices to help you make an upgrade from a less ideal choice to a better choice. Remember to ask this question whenever a tempting situation comes up.

Day 18: Handling the Things That Hold You Back

Yesterday we addressed ways to overcome your own behaviors that hold you back. Yet, what about the big obstacles that are outside yourself? Time constraints and money issues are usually the two biggest factors. However, there is a third, hidden cause of sabotage that is often overlooked - the fear of losing the approval of others.

For habits that have a social component, the desire for approval can be a big motivating factor either supporting or hindering your habit development. We're hardwired to be social creatures. Being rejected by the "tribe" is a threat to your very survival from a biological point of view. As emotional creatures, we're often more tempted to do what's cool than what's smart.

This shows up when a person fears going to the gym because they're worried about looking like an idiot. A person may hesitate to bring a healthy lunch to work because their co-workers will mock them for being a health nut. A person who worries about expressing appreciation and admiration may fear looking like a suck-up.

It's also possible to worry about what others will think of you after your new habit leads to significant changes in your life. The mental conversation goes like this; "If I start making more money or get in better shape, will people think I'm too good for them? I don't want to come across as better than anyone else. I better stick with where I'm at." You might not even be *conscious* of this conversation in your head, but it's still taking place deep down in your brain where your beliefs are stored.

Before addressing a solution to this, let's take a look at the other common reasons people have for not upgrading their habits – lack of time or money. While these may be excuses to save face from a deeper concern a person has, such as losing approval, these challenges can and are often very real obstacles to overcome.

If we address time first, we can see that the problem is never a lack of time. As long as a person says, "I don't have enough time," they'll never be able to solve the problem because it's *literally* impossible to get more time. The real truth is this person has other things they're prioritizing more than what they say they don't have time for. The more accurate statement is, "I am prioritizing other things more than this thing."

With money, taking a note from Anthony Robbins, often it's not so much a lack of resources as much as a lack of *resourcefulness* that is the problem. There were times where I couldn't afford attending a high-end seminar to grow my business, but I was able to volunteer as a crew member and still get the lessons. There are libraries full of free information. There are people willing to trade services. There are countless options that don't require money if you're *resourceful.*

You have to get to the real problem before you can come up with a real solution.

The good news is, the way to find the solution is relatively simple. Not always *easy*, but simple. A way to unlock your creative problem-solving ability is by asking a question rather than making a statement.

Instead of, "I don't have time," it's really "How can I change my schedule to set aside the time?" or "What am I prioritizing more than this that I don't need to?" Instead of, "I can't because I don't have enough money," it's "What else can I do instead?" or "How can I find a way?"

When it comes to the influences of others, it's also a matter of choosing your priorities. "Would I rather let these people have power over me to dictate how I live my life, OR can I just give myself approval to do what I know is going to make me far happier in the long run?"

For me, it's usually simple enough to ask, "Do I want this person (these people) to have power over me?" The answer is often no, and I'm *usually* able to get focused back on the fact that I'd rather be the one in control of my life instead of handing that control over to others by letting their opinion sway me.

You probably won't completely overcome all of the fears in your life instantly. Rather, what you'll notice is that these questions help you take one small step to stretch, not break, your comfort zone. As you get used to acting in spite of being a *little* uncomfortable, what you're comfortable with expands. Eventually, you may be doing things that used to scare you to death without much, if any, trepidation.

Another more obvious solution is to reduce your time spent around negative influences, and increase your time spent around people who inspire you to be better. Remember from earlier, environment is stronger than willpower. If your environment is hurting you, can you just take one small step to improve your influences? This may not mean you can completely cut out bad influences, but could you just increase the presence of good influences by listening and reading more uplifting material?

Recap

- A hidden cause of sabotage is worrying about what others will think.
- Lack of time isn't a real problem, it's how you manage your priorities. Lack of money doesn't need to stop you from taking a forward step if you're resourceful.
- Ask questions about what's possible rather than make statements about what's impossible.
- It's not about an instant solution, but rather taking steps to get you moving forward.

Action Steps
1. Ask yourself, "What's my lesson from this?"
2. Ask yourself, "What external factors in my life hold me back?"
3. Consider, "If I knew a way to overcome this, what would it be?"
4. Create a "Would I rather?" question based around the external limiter and the healthy habit.

Example:
1. "I'm so busy that I don't have enough time."
2. "I can cut out all non-work related web browsing during the day to free up an extra twenty minutes a day to devote to my reading habit."
3. "Would I rather waste time browsing the web which won't provide me any real long-term benefits OR can I just take those twenty minutes to read a book to stimulate my mind, learn new skills, and help me reach my long-term goals?"

Day 19: Visualizing 2.0

Right now we've been using a small amount of willpower to get moving forward with your micro-habit. What do you do in situations, such as training yourself to wake up as soon as the alarm goes off, where your conscious effort isn't strong enough?

Steve Pavlina faced this same issue, and his solution is genius. Later in the day, *while fully awake*, he would practice lying in bed, having the alarm go off, taking a full breath, and getting up out of bed quickly. He was able to practice this easily while in a more fully conscious state to train his subconscious mind to respond to the cue of the alarm going off to engage in the routine of getting out of bed right away. See his article for more details here: http://www.stevepavlina.com/blog/2006/04/how-to-get-up-right-away-when-your-alarm-goes-off

This method is similar to how I would visualize myself and even act out being a confident, engaging stage performer while in my room practicing guitar. If I waited until I stepped out on stage to practice giving a good performance, then A) I'd have fewer practice opportunities because I didn't perform often and B) I'd be fighting some nervousness. However, by visualizing and practicing in a "safe" environment, I was able to train myself to perform well even under pressure.

Regardless of the type of habit you're developing, the act of visualizing yourself doing it, succeeding at it, and best of all *enjoying* it helps give you brain more mental repetitions to ingrain a habit even deeper.

This type of visualization is different than when people simply visualize themselves being successful and getting the *results*. While this type of positive visualization can be helpful in its own way, for habit development, you'll want to visualize yourself engaged in the *process* and overcoming obstacles.

I could also visualize myself waking up in the morning and making a smoothie as soon as I step into the kitchen. I'm training my brain to associate "step into kitchen (cue)" with "make smoothie (routine)" each time I visualize, thus allowing me to reinforce the habit multiple times per day.

I can even use visualization to create *mental habits*, like the habit of pushing through the discomfort of exercise. Before running a sprint at a track workout, I could visualize myself going around the track, imagine that feeling of wanting to quit towards the latter half, and then see myself pushing through the pain and keeping my form solid. This type of visualization is helpful on its own, but obviously it should still be combined with actually performing the act itself.

Recap

- Practicing a habit in a controlled environment helps increase performance when in a different state.
- Visualizing can be a mental form of practice. It's very helpful to visualize yourself facing challenges you might actually face and seeing yourself overcome them.
- You can speed up your rate of success by visualizing and practicing throughout the day.

Action Step

1. Ask yourself, "What's my lesson from this?"
2. At any time during the day, and ideally before falling asleep at night, take a few moments to visualize yourself successfully engaging in your habit. If there's a particular aspect of your habit that's challenging, see yourself succeeding at it effortlessly.

Day 20: The Fool-Proof Way to Always Find Your Next Step

While most of this book has been focused on overcoming the internal battle of how to improve your habits, there's one obvious issue – what if you don't know how to take things to the next level?

If someone is striving to transform their physical health and they start with a pushup a day, eventually they're going to get to a point where they don't know what else to do. They need *specialized knowledge* such as a workout plan designed to help them reach their fitness goals.

I purposely saved addressing this towards the end because I want you to see for yourself just how much you can do to start improving your habits. That being said, there will come a point where you do need knowledge that you might not currently have. It may even be counter-productive to keep doing more without specialized knowledge.

A perfect example of this is when I taught guitar students who had been practicing with poor technique. All of their hard work was actually reinforcing bad habits. This meant that not only were they wasting their time, but they were doing more harm than good.

The problem is the students didn't *know* they had bad technique. It took an *outsider* who had greater perspective and understanding to point it out. This is exactly why coaches or mentors are crucial to your success.

The shortcut to success is to find another successful person and learn from them.

While you can get good coaching from a book, video series, or some other form of media, some habits that have more skill involved would benefit from a real life, third-party perspective in the form of a coach or guide. Having a guide can also be beneficial because, if they're good, they know exactly what you need to work on and when. They can see the bigger picture so you don't waste your time with things that may be important, but not important right *now*. As Anthony Robbins says, "Most people fail because they major in minor things." A coach keeps you focused on the most critical things for your success.

Don't let the idea of a guide make you think you need to hire someone that's around all the time. This can also refer to simply asking for advice from someone you know with knowledge in an area. This is surprisingly rare in my experience. I was talking to a guy who wanted to take up biking. I asked him what was holding him back, and he said he didn't know what kind of bike equipment to get. I asked him something like, "If there was someone who knew what kind of bike could be good for you, who would it be?" He quickly responded, "My aunt!" He then went on to say he could call her and she would be able to help him out because she knows a lot about biking. He had the answer all along, but what was really holding him back was he didn't think to look for a guide to help him with his challenge until he was forced to think about it by my question.

While this may be common sense for a person like you who's smart enough to be reading this book, what is important to remember is that it's not enough to find something that simply works. That's because there are *a lot* of things that can work to achieve a desired result. The real challenge is *sticking with a plan long enough* to see it through rather than jumping from one program to another.

Two common things I see as a fitness coach are people hopping from one workout program or diet to another every couple weeks. As someone who has coached entrepreneurs, I also see people hop from one business plan to another without ever sticking with one thing long enough to see results. This is commonly known as "shiny object syndrome."

Shiny object syndrome also takes on a more subtle form though, and this form has sabotaged me countless times. This is something I will dub "eager tweaker syndrome," in which a person is too eager to tweak, modify, and get creative with a proven plan. For a person with this condition, everything has to be upgraded or changed in some way – even before trying it out as-is to begin with. It's particularly challenging for creative types to overcome because we're hardwired to look for ways to improve things even if they don't need improving.

Innovation is great. However, it's important to realize innovation comes *later* in the process. Go for proven before innovation. Don't reinvent the wheel until it's necessary, and it's rarely necessary.

If this describes you at all, then realize that from the start of a planned program, you may get bored or scared that there's something better out there, and there probably is. The question is, "Would you rather search endlessly for the best plan ever only to not stick with anything long enough to benefit you, or can you just find one thing that's been proven to be effective and be at peace knowing it will get you to where you want to be?"

How do you find a proven plan? I'll offer some resources at the end to help with a few major habits that often come up for people such as fitness, productivity, and stress relief. However, like most things, you probably already know the answer, or at least the next step in *finding* the answer. You'll simply need to unleash your creativity with a few powerful questions.

Recap
- Experts are your shortcut to success.
- Sometimes you need real life outsider perspective to see your blind spots.
- Go with what's proven before innovating, and stick with

it long enough to see it through. Remember, some things can take a while and have a learning curve before you see tangible benefits.

Action Steps

1. Ask yourself, "What's my lesson from this?"
2. Ask yourself, "What is a proven way to make my habit even better?"
3. "Who can offer guidance to make my habit even better?"
4. Do one thing to take advantage of these resources today.

If you're still having trouble, here are some creativity unleashing questions.

- "Who do I know that's good at this? How can I contact them?"
- "Who might know *someone else* that's good at this?"
- "If in five years I have this all figured out, what would I go back in time and tell myself now?"
- "What's my next step to take to start researching and exploring a potential solution?"

Day 21: What to Do When You Want Bigger, Better, Faster Results

At this point, you've built the foundation for a healthy habit that will last you a lifetime. Take a moment to congratulate yourself and think about how far you've come. Even though your healthy habit may not be fully ingrained just yet, if you keep doing what you've learned, which only takes a few minutes a day, you can be assured that you'll be even more successful over the long run.

Let's look at all you've learned. You know how to remind yourself of your habit with a cue you've set up. You realize that momentum creates motivation, and momentum can be generated with micro-habits. You know how to overcome overwhelm by asking yourself, "Can I just?" and picking a too-easy-to-not-do action. You're able to take your habit to the next level by getting both external and internal feedback by asking yourself and mentors, "How can I make this even better?" Finally, you understand the critical and often missing piece of the puzzle, which is changing your identity to match your new habit.

Up to this point I've been keeping the focus on the process rather than the results. Today's lesson, however, is focused on how you can get results at the quickest possible rate while incorporating everything you've learned about mastering the habit development process.

You can ignore today's lesson if you're happy with the gradual approach and don't feel you need to get better results extra fast. This isn't for everyone because it will likely require breaking the five minutes a day approach we've been doing up to this point.

If, however, you're willing to invest and commit more to transforming your life, and you want to see things happen quickly, then this can be worthwhile to know. I'm going to share with you the method that I've seen transform people's lives quickly *if they apply everything else taught in this book along with it.*

That one thing is to take on a challenge, usually in the form of a 21-90 day challenge. As you know, you've already done a mini-challenge by going through this book. Can you see how effective this challenge approach is?

Since you've laid the foundation for developing habits, you can now take on a bigger challenge that will stretch your comfort zone and require a greater investment of time and sometimes even of money.

Examples of some challenges people engage in offline or online are:

- Signing up and training for a marathon, 5k, triathlon, or other fitness-related event.
- Writing a book in 30 days.
- Reading for 30 minutes a day for 90 days.
- Meditating for 30 minutes a day for 30 days.
- Doing a workout program for 90 days.
- Cutting out junk food for 30 days.

Obviously, your options are limitless. Some of these challenges have an element of accountability to them in that they can be done in a group setting. One reason some people sign up for a marathon is because they know they will be forced to show up and therefore must train regularly for it. They're even more accountable if they sign up with friends and all train together.

There's also another aspect that helps people follow through with a challenge. This thing is why people get addicted to gambling and stay in bad relationships. Put simply, they can require you to invest in something. Once a person has put a good portion of time, money, and/or emotions into something, they'll be less likely to want to quit.

When someone spends a few hundred dollars on a personal trainer or fitness program for instance, they'll usually want to get their money's worth by following through. This is why when people simply rely on free YouTube fitness videos, which are still valuable, there's a much greater chance they won't follow through because they haven't *invested* into it.

Finally, challenges are a great way to benefit from extrinsic rewards. Some challenges offer cash prizes and awards, but you can also add in your own rewards for successfully completing a challenge. You'll notice that I have a reward for you for completing the Healthy Habit Revolution Challenge.

An ideal challenge will:

- Hold you accountable to others or a deadline.
- Make you put something on the line and/or require *upfront* investment.
- Will test your limits, therefore giving you a *huge* sense of accomplishment for following through.
- Provide a big payoff in either internal feelings of pride or external benefits like winning a prize, completing a project, or being in better shape.

I run free healthy habits challenge groups on Facebook, as well as special fitness challenge groups to provide accountability and support. See http://upgradeyourhabits.com/challenge for more details. There are also plenty of other resources out there for challenge groups that you can find with just a little bit of research and resourcefulness.

Recap

- Once the foundation of habit development is in place, you can step things up to take on a bigger challenge.
- Challenges help provide accountability, a big sense of accomplishment, and a big payoff.

Action Steps

Today's action steps are only required if you want to take things even further faster by engaging in a challenge.

1. Ask yourself, "What's my lesson from this?"
2. Ask yourself, "What would challenge me and create a breakthrough result in my life?"
3. "Where can I find a group to do this?" or "Who would know where to find a challenge for my goal?" "How can I create a challenge for myself with this and stay accountable?"

Hint: Meetup.com can be a great way to find like-minded people interested in your healthy habit who may already have or are willing to create a challenge group. Stickk. com is a way to find an accountability partner and create a challenge for yourself.

Revealing the Hidden Lessons

Congratulations! You've made it through the 21-day Healthy Habit Revolution Challenge! You should be feeling pretty badass right now. Take a moment to thank yourself for doing something to make your life even more incredible.

If you slipped up a few days, or even a lot, and yet you still made it here, you should be extra proud of yourself because that means you got back on track – a critical quality to developing better habits and improving your life. Hopefully you learned from any slip-ups so you can do even better going forward.

Ideally, you will be running through this again to develop more great habits. Once your current habit becomes mostly automatic, you can go back to day four and repeat the process again with a new habit. You'll be happy to know that any mistakes you made the first time, if learned from, will work in your favor so you can be more prepared the next time through.

Throughout these past few weeks, I've been strategically taking you through a process. Within this process there are a few hidden lessons and things you've been cultivating perhaps without even realizing it.

One habit you've been developing is the habit of recognizing and changing your language patterns. The reason this is crucial is because you will always have an inner critic, which is a part of the ego, telling you you're not good enough, comparing yourself to others, and giving you plenty of reasons not to move forward.

This is normal and natural. A lot of people try to do one of two things when they learn about this. They either try to eliminate this part of themselves, *or* they doom themselves to being a helpless victim of it. Neither of these approaches work.

The problem with trying to eliminate it is that you simply can't. It's built into you, and it will always be there. The real key is to acknowledge where it's coming from, and make a *choice* to either align your actions to it or to something greater.

For instance, whenever I'm writing a book such as this one, I'm dealing with more than just changing my writing habits. I'm confronting a voice that says, "Who do you think you are, writing this book? No one wants to hear this. This sucks! Other people are way smarter than you, and you should just let them get the message out there. Just go watch kittens play on YouTube, and worry about this nonsense later."

Since I can't get rid of this voice, I must understand it. "Oh, that's the voice of my ego. Thanks for sharing, however, I'm going to choose to listen to the part of me that says I have a mission to share with others the things that have helped me."

As a mentor of mine, Brandon Broader, has pointed out, this ego is actually serving a useful purpose. It's to empower the higher part of ourselves. This resistance gives you something to work against. It's like a weight that, when lifted, makes you stronger. If you didn't face any challenges or obstacles, internal or external, how would you get stronger and develop yourself?

Remember that growth is one of the six human needs, and growth *requires* confronting and overcoming what you're not comfortable with. Every time you overcome your inner critic, you build your willpower and inner strength. That means that it's not an enemy, but a potential ally to upgrading yourself.

"Everything can either serve or enslave you depending on how you respond to it." – Derek Doepker

What you have been developing through this book is the habit of not fighting against your resistance, but acknowledging it and turning it into a choice. The "Would I rather?" approach is really asking, "Would I rather give into fear *or* would I rather have faith and trust?" Your success will depend on taking ongoing leaps of faith and having trust that things can work out.

Another critical lesson is that successful people start moving forward before they see the entire path. Hopefully, you had a certain confidence that this Derek guy knows what he's talking about so you could take action each day without knowing what it was leading to in the long run. In real life, you don't have the luxury of knowing that someone's laid out a path for you. That means we often try to see the entire path *before* starting. Our fear says if we're not prepared for everything that's coming up, we shouldn't even begin.

Yet, this is a completely *impossible* approach. You'll never see the entire path ahead of time. Even if you could, by the time you get halfway there, something will have changed, and you'll need to take a detour. All you really need to see is the *next* step, and *then* you'll be given more clarity and insight. It's like driving a car at night where you can only see what's right in front of you. While only seeing a few feet ahead, you can drive hundreds or thousands of miles. Not seeing what's a mile down the road is no reason to stop you from driving the next fifty feet and trusting you'll find where to go from there.

Another thing you've heard me emphasize quite a lot is the concept of momentum, and momentum is generated from small acts. It's the little things that will lead to either an upward or downward spiral. The decision to do one minute of exercise can, in the long-run, lead to an increase in momentum that completely transforms your body years from now. By the same token, the decision to skip that exercise could lead to a loss of momentum that also transforms your body years from now, but not in a good way.

One of my favorite examples of a downward spiral is the show Breaking Bad. One compromise in morals leads to going deeper and deeper down a rabbit hole of lies, violence, and terrible consequences.

I know for myself that once I make one compromise, it potentially sets a precedent that compromise in general is OK, and the next thing I know, days, weeks, or months down the road, I could be in a far worse condition without any idea about how things could have gotten so bad. Looking back, it was usually one tiny compromise that set a precedent for everything that followed.

This goes back to the process vs. result concept. If we focus on how something will affect the results, small daily decisions don't make a big difference. Eating a salad one day for lunch will not make or break a person's health. Yet, when you look at it from a *process* perspective, the decision whether or not to align to what someone says they're going to do, like eating a salad for lunch, will affect their *momentum*. This is especially important because a single compromise, such as "I'll just eat one donut," can occasionally result in what Janet Polivy refers to as the "what-the-hell" effect in which the person says, "What the hell! I've already messed up my diet today, so I'll just indulge and start fresh tomorrow."

The point here is that one good decision, no matter how small, can lead to more good decisions. One poor decision, *no matter how small*, can lead to things far worse. The very outcome of your life could very well depend on the smallest seemingly inconsequential decisions you make, not on the big life-altering choices. As mentioned earlier, this doesn't mean you can't have the occasional treat or pleasure. The important thing is to be aware of how your decisions affect your momentum.

This all comes down to cultivating an identity that says, "I'm a person who does the right thing and sticks with my commitments, even when it's hard. I'm a person who values the process as much as the results. I value my integrity more than the outcome."

If you've made it this far, you know you have these qualities already. Plus, you have one more important skill – the ability to develop better habits. With the things you've learned, you've created a foundation for upgrading your entire life to a whole new level! How cool is that?

There's one final lesson though, and it comes with a warning. What I'm about to say is quite possibly the ultimate paradox. It's something I don't think most people who talk about habits take the time to mention.

I'm going to reveal how habits, even good habits, can actually be destructive and harmful. Remember, *everything*, including the best habits, can either serve or enslave you.

How can good habits be a bad thing? The answer is that you must avoid becoming so inflexible with them that you can't see if they become counter-productive. Good habits can be destructive if done at the wrong time or when out of balance with other good habits.

A person in the habit of pushing themselves to their max during exercise may get great results, but done at the wrong time could lead to injury if they're not being mindful of whether this habit is serving or enslaving them at that moment. A person may get in the habit of meditating every morning, but there could come a time where something is more important that morning, like calling a family member to check up on them, and they need to be mindful *not* to engage in their habit that day. Using a harmless example, have you ever had a server ask you, "How's your meal?" and you respond unthinkingly out of habit with, "Great! How about you?" This is because you were running on autopilot and not truly present to the moment.

Another problem is when people get obsessed over their habits and identity. For instance, a person can go to the *extreme* of being a healthy eater, and then they have a panic attack when the food they want isn't available. They live in fear and stress about not being the healthiest person ever. The ironic thing is that stressing out about making the healthiest choices is probably *more* damaging than just eating some junk food to begin with!

There's almost always a context in which a good habit can backfire. Clearly then, good habits aren't the ultimate thing we're after. There must be something even more significant than your habits that will determine your success. The ultimate secret of this book is to cultivate that thing greater than your habits so you're *not* always driven by them.

What is that ultimate thing we're after?

Mindfulness. Presence. Mindful Awareness. Whatever you want to call it, it's all the same concept. Being conscious of your choices and not being a slave to living your life on autopilot. Living in the moment to make a conscientious decision about how a choice will either help or hurt you right now. Not being stuck with only one approach, but having flexibility to adapt to whatever circumstances you're in.

You see, habits are actually a *result*. The true beauty of developing habits is that, in the early stages, it *requires* more mindful awareness. It's cultivating mindfulness that is the ultimate "habit," if you will, and it will be the thing that sets you *free* from habits – at least when they're not serving you.

"What you get by achieving your goals is not nearly as important as what you become by achieving them." - Zig Ziglar

In this case, the goal is developing better habits, but who you become is a person who is more mindful of your thoughts, feelings, and actions. This is critical for not only developing good habits, but it's the thing that will help you break bad habits *as well as* temporarily break good habits when they won't serve you in a particular situation. As they say, it's about the journey and not the destination. The journey is about becoming ever more present and conscious.

Since the journey never ends, where do you go from here? Your next step is to continue to educate and develop yourself. If you remember, a big key to my early health success was reading and studying about health and nutrition. I've found that the more I'm reading about a topic and studying it, the more it keeps it in the forefront of my mind.

This book is a double-edged sword. It's very action oriented and gives you a quick overview of principles, but it may leave you feeling like you want even more information on the science of habits, examples from other people, and more. Continue reading the next section of the book to get more helpful resources for ongoing education and learning.

5 Absurdly Simple Habits That Will Change Your Life

It should come as no surprise that the habits that will have the biggest impact on your life are typically things you probably already know will benefit you. Throughout this book, I've kept my examples of healthy habits fairly limited. I mostly talk about exercising, meditating, reading, eating healthier foods, being productive, and expressing gratitude.

The reason?

I believe these are some of the most powerful keystone habits. Keystone habits, if you remember, are habits that will tend to lead to positive changes in many areas of life. For instance, exercising makes you feel better, improves your health, and builds your confidence. As a result, many people who start exercising want to take their results even further by eating better foods, drinking more water, and getting adequate sleep.

The benefits of intense exercise can go beyond just improving physical health however. I've found my ability to push myself with exercise trained my willpower to push through other uncomfortable areas of life. I can approach the challenges life throws my way as simply a form of "resistance" to overcome and develop my inner strength.

Exercise helps me develop the mentality of a champion athlete which has also transformed me into a champion entrepreneur, writer, and friend.

Can you see how this one single habit of exercise can dramatically improve seemingly unrelated things like my relationships and finances as a side-effect?

All parts of your life are interconnected. What's happening in your personal relationships will affect your work, play, and health. What's happening at work will affect your relationships, health, and happiness. You get the idea. We can't isolate the impact of a single habit to just one area of life.

The following five habits are things that I believe can create a ripple effect that makes almost everything at least a little bit better. There are certainly far more than five keystone habits. Use this list as a helpful guide, and feel free to expand upon it with your own healthy habits that suit your goals and lifestyle.

Habit 1 – Meditation

I'll admit, sometimes I lose sight of why I meditate. I'm just sitting there doing nothing. Then I have to consider the transformational changes that have happened to me over the past couple of years. Is my newfound ability to be significantly more productive, see things from many perspectives, and quickly regain inner peace after a stressful experience stemming from my meditation practice? What else could have shifted in my inner emotional life so profoundly over the past couple of years?

From personal experience and the avalanche of scientific studies coming out showing the benefits of meditation, I'm pretty sure I can say it was meditation that played a significant part in upgrading my life. Meditation has been shown to create long lasting changes in the way the brain functions.

Meditation leads to benefits like living more in the now, improving mood, increasing resilience to stress, shifting to a solution-focused mindset, enhancing your immune system, and a lot more. It's even been shown to shrink part of the Amygdala, the area of the brain responsible for producing fear. *Source: (Taren AA)*

Best of all, it doesn't take lifetime of meditation to achieve benefits. There has been research showing brain changes start to take place after as little as five hours of total meditation over the course of several weeks.

Source: (Moyer CA) Isn't it worth a few minutes of your day to see benefits in virtually *every* area of your life?

I view meditation as rehab for the brain. Just like you can fix physical pain by strengthening muscles surrounding a joint, you can fix *psychological* and emotional pain by strengthening and altering certain connections in your brain. If you value exercise for your physical muscles, then consider meditation to be the equally essential exercise for your psychological and emotional "muscles."

Steps for Practicing Mindful Meditation

Mindfulness meditation is simply the act of bringing your conscious awareness completely into the present moment. You'll observe your thoughts and feelings in a non-judgmental way, and refocus your attention to something like your breath.

Here's how to do it:

- Sit in a relaxed, upright position with your spine straight, and feet flat on the floor. Alternatively, if you're comfortable in a seated meditation position, you may do that.
- Start to *focus* on your breath going in and out. Whenever your mind wanders, and it will, simply allow your focus to return to your breath going in and out. The actual act of refocusing your attention is part of the process training yourself to stay present. So it's OK if you find yourself having to refocus quite a bit.
- If it helps you relax, you can mentally "scan" your body head to toe relaxing each muscle and body part.
- Continue this for 1-15 minutes (start with just a few minutes daily), or as long as you're comfortable.
- As you get more proficient at being able to focus only on your breath during meditation, you may begin to simply observe your thoughts coming and going. Rather than fight any thoughts because you find them distracting

from the meditation, simply watch them pass through your awareness. It can help to think of yourself not as "me" or "my thoughts," but as an overall awareness of those things. You can ask yourself, "Am I these thoughts, or am I that which is aware of these thoughts?" As you do this, you'll find you more naturally let them go.

While the purpose of meditation isn't necessarily to try to stop all thoughts but rather observe them, if you really want to quiet your mind, you may mentally make the effort to watch for the next thought that is going to occur. Interestingly enough, the more you try to watch for the next thought to arise, the fewer thoughts seem to come, until your mind becomes quiet and still.

Even though meditation is an *active* process, don't worry about "screwing it up." Remember, as long as you do it regularly with focused intent, even if your mind wonders a lot at first, you'll start to get better.

Suggested Micro-Habit
Meditate for 30 seconds a day.

Suggested Upgrades
Mediate for up to 5-60 minutes per day.
Use brainwave entrainment (see details below).
Use guided meditations (see details below).
Explore various meditation practices such as mindfulness meditation and focused meditation.

Resources
My current meditation practice incorporates brainwave entrainment technology to enhance the experience and for added benefits. There are a number of good companies offering brainwave entrainment from Hemi-Sync, The Morry Method, and the company I personally use the most - iAwake.

You can learn more and get a free track from iAwake here: http://excuseproof.com/iawake

https://www.headspace.com/headspace-meditation-app - Head Space offers a free meditation app.

http://marc.ucla.edu/body.cfm?id=22 – UCLA Mindful Awareness Research Center offers free guided audio meditations.

http://www.heartmath.org/free-services/downloads/de-stress-kit-for-the-changing-times.html - While not strictly about meditation, HeartMath is doing cutting edge research on heart rate coherence and stress. By measuring Heart Rate Variability, they're able to determine a person's level of "coherence." Greater coherence means less stress, more happiness, and improved health. Using specialized breathing exercises, one can increase their level of coherence. Learn more about their research at HeartMath.org

Habit 2 – Reading, Studying, and Applying Personal Development

There's a good chance you already know the value of this habit, otherwise you wouldn't be reading this book. That being said, there's one thing I want to point out, and that is exposing myself to a *wide variety* of topics in the realm of personal development has given me more insight than just focusing on a single topic that I'm struggling with.

What do I mean?

Let's say I'm struggling to develop better habits. While reading books on that topic will be helpful, reading books on the topics of influence, productivity, and health can all help me with habit development even if they're not directly related. Much of the insight in this book comes from research into a wide range of topics.

Just like there are keystone habits, there's what I call keystone knowledge. For instance, learning influence skills will help you influence yourself, motivate others which can lead to business and parenting success, and can even keep you from getting scammed by someone using those skills in an unethical way because you know the "tricks."

A person may think they need a book on business success, but in reality they may need a book on relationship success in order to make a breakthrough in their business. That's because their perceived problem, a business that's struggling, may actually have its root in something else – a relationship at home that's struggling. Can you see how studying a wide range of topics can have an impact in every area of life?

This also means studying a topic from multiple angles. While obviously you should totally go out and read every single book I've ever published, don't limit yourself to my work just because you love how awesome, charming, and incredible I am. Give other people a shot too. In all seriousness, seeing things from multiple perspectives is essential to developing a well-rounded approach to any issue.

At the same time, you'll need to watch out for getting so many different conflicting ideas that your head is spinning. This is a balancing act, and you already know how to deal with it. Subtract to get started, then slowly add more information to improve. Take things with a grain of salt and don't believe everything you read – not even from me.

While I believe in the value of actually sitting down and reading, there's something to be said for books on tape, podcasts, and other forms of personal development. I particularly enjoy live trainings which have had the biggest transformational effect on me. Feel free to reach out and learn more about some of my mentors and what I recommend based on your goals by contacting me at derek@upgradeyourhabits.com

Suggested Micro-Habit
Read one page of a personal development book a day.

Suggested Upgrades
- Read 5 – 20 pages a day or 1 – 2 chapters.
- Read topics that are unconventional or new for you.
- Listen to personal development while driving, cleaning, or exercising.

Resources
Here are some recommended books that cover a lot of ground:
How To Win Friends And Influence People by Dale Carnegie – A

must read for managing one of your life's greatest assets, your relationship with others.

The Sedona Method by Hale Dwoskin – What you need to know about managing your emotions and overcoming fear, anxiety, and resistance.

The Success Principles by Jack Canfield and Janet Switzer – The most descriptive and all inclusive book on what it takes to be successful in any area of life.

The Heartmath Solution by Doc Childre, Howard Martin, and Donna Beech – Discover the impact your heart has on the brain and learn stress management techniques to restore health and well-being.

Why You're Stuck by Derek Doepker – What I've learned from 10 years of researching the world's top coaches, psychologists, and personal development experts on how to identify and overcome any of life's challenges.

50 Fitness Tips You Wish You Knew by Derek Doepker – Discover my top 50 tips to hack your brain and body for unstoppable motivation and superhuman fitness.

Note: You can find more recommended books in the resources section.

Habit 3 – Physical Health Habits

Being a fitness coach, obviously I believe physical health is pretty important. That being said, some people may get the wrong idea about why I value the physical body so much. I had a friend, who admired my talent for both music composition and writing, ask me why I was so into fitness. It seemed vain and like a waste of time to him.

I explained that health and fitness isn't just about walking around with a six pack and looking good, although that's nice. It's also not about adding a few extra years to the end of my life. Instead, it's about feeling great *right now*. It's about how taking care of my body enhances my creativity and productivity in everything else I do like writing books and music. It's also about training myself mentally to push through perceived limitations and see that I'm capable of more than I may have originally thought I was capable of.

I truly believe those that prioritize their health and fitness are much more likely to succeed in other areas of life. That's not to say someone can't be incredibly successful and treat their body terribly, but oftentimes their success is short-lived and limited to a specific area of talent. I've seen those that take care of their body often find they develop discipline, confidence, and extra energy to tackle whatever life throws their way. In the mind/body/spirit equation, the body is essential for maximizing the potential of the mind and spirit.

There are three key areas of physical health:

1. Sleep
2. Nutrition
3. Exercise

Since this is my area of expertise, and one topic that requires some personalization depending on a person's goals, feel free to contact me at derek@upgradeyourhabits.com if you'd like some guidance on picking a nutrition and workout plan.

Generally speaking, if I have one recommendation with physical health that people may not initially know the value of, it would be to incorporate intense resistance training. This can often be overlooked by women who fear adding too much muscle. On the contrary, it's often the missing link to losing stubborn fat and reshaping the body. From a non-appearance standpoint, resistance training has been shown to have some of the most significant health benefits of any type of exercise. Keep in mind resistance training can include body-weight exercises and isn't limited to weights. There are many highly effective at-home workout routines for those who don't have access to a gym.

There is technically a fourth and potentially most critical aspect of health, and that is stress. You can read more about reducing stress through the work of Doc Orman.

For the following suggestions, remember you only want to focus on one thing during a 21-day challenge. As you get comfortable with the process, you may choose to adjust up to three things at a time if the changes are small. For now, you may simply pick from one of the areas of health and focus on one small improvement in that area.

Suggested Micro-Habits
Sleep:
*   10-20 minutes before bed, give yourself time away from computer and TV screens. I suggest reading during this time to help the body relax.

Nutrition:
*   Make a green juice or superfood smoothie every morning.

- Add one vegetable to a meal. *For example, eat a piece of celery at dinner.*
- Drink a glass of water upon waking.
- Swap one snack with a piece of fruit.

Exercise:
- Do one set of a resistance exercise per day. For example, do one set of pushups. You may reduce to a single rep if that's too challenging.
- Do one minute of any physical activity such as walking.

Suggested Upgrades
Sleep:
- Schedule at least seven hours of sleep every night.

Nutrition:
- Eat at least one healthy meal each day that's made from scratch. Note: I prefer to cook in bulk once or twice a week and save the leftovers.
- Add a serving of vegetables to every meal. Note: Also easier if prepared in bulk.
- Carry a container of water with you everywhere you go. Note: Over-hydration exists. Simply drink when thirsty.
- Replace sugary snacks and drinks with fruit.

Exercise:
- Engage in 10 – 60 minutes of intense resistance training.
- Engage in 5 – 30 minutes of cardiovascular training.

Resources
ExcuseProof.com
JCDFitness.com
T-Nation.com

Habit 4 – Daily Gratitude

We all know we should count our blessings. A couple years ago if someone told me about gratitude being good for me, I would have been like, "Yeah, I know. Gratitude is great. Now what's the *real* secret to happiness?" It's just not one of those sexy topics that really captivates your attention. Or at least we think we're really embracing the concept while leaving a lot on the table.

I want you to try something right now that will hopefully wake you up to the power of gratitude. Imagine for a moment that you're in a poor, destitute country. Your body is writhing with pain from sickness, hunger, and thirst. You don't have the luxury of seeing or hearing. You have few if any friends and family, and those you do know are suffering as well. You see no hope for a bright future. All you know is pain and misery. All you can do is pray for a miracle to be free from this suffering.

Got it? Really take a moment to let this experience sink in. Pause for a moment here and feel what life would be like in these conditions.

Now imagine a miracle has been granted and you've woken up to your current life. You've traded all that suffering in for whatever inconveniences you currently have which probably seem pretty minor. For myself as a musician, I think how amazing it is that I can listen to music now since before I couldn't hear. I get to have a comfortable bed to sleep in. I get to have a body that's mostly free from pain. I can eat when I'm hungry. I have friends and family that love me. I have a car to drive, a roof that keeps me protected from the elements, a computer that connects me with people from all around the world, a vast world of knowledge at my fingertips, people I can count on if I'm in trouble, the knowledge to find solutions to my challenges, a fit body that can lift heavy things, my ability to write and play music, and so on. That's just a stream of consciousness list of things that swell my heart with joy if I only take a moment to reflect on what I'm grateful for.

It doesn't matter whether or not you can think of *a lot* of things to be grateful for right now. For now, if you really think about it, do you have *something* you can be grateful for that you haven't really considered? Is there something you overlook each day, such as the ability to read a book, which makes your life even better?

I'm not saying gratitude practices will make everything in your life sunshine and rainbows. I'm definitely not saying you have to pretend everything is OK and "just be grateful." It's okay to think things kind of suck. For the time being, simply see if you can allow yourself to think, "I don't like some things in my life, *but* I'm so grateful for…"

The true power of gratitude happens not just when you consider what you're grateful for, but when you express to others what you appreciate about them. Writing thank you cards to my parents for all they did to me growing up not only brought them joy, but it made me tear up with joy just writing the cards. That's because the research on gratitude shows when you give gratitude to others, not only do you enhance their health and happiness, it actually improves *your* health and happiness. In other words, when you *give* happiness you *receive* it too. Wouldn't you like to do something that makes *everyone's* life better?

You'll find giving regular appreciation, which many people are starving to receive, enhances relationships too. Imagine how much better your relationships with a partner, friends, family, co-workers, and even strangers would be if you're showering them on a regular basis with *genuine* appreciation. Make it a habit, and don't be surprised just how many things in life just seem to automatically start improving because of this one foundational habit.

One caveat here is that this must be genuine and done without an expectation of getting appreciation in return. This shouldn't be a "I'll give appreciation so people appreciate me" type of thing. It's also not about kissing ass to suck up to people. You'll know you're doing it right when you feel good giving appreciation to others without needing to even hear anything back from them.

Suggested Micro-Habit

- Ask yourself daily, "What is one thing I'm grateful for? What is one thing I *should* be grateful for that I haven't considered recently?"

Suggested Upgrade

- Tell one person everyday something you're grateful they did with an example. For instance – "I really appreciate the way you took your time to ask me if there was anything I needed from the store. It shows how considerate you are and I want you to know it means a lot to me."
- Write a thank you note each day, which can be an email or text message if necessary, expressing your appreciation for something someone did. Also remember it's okay if it's a small thing. Have you ever wished someone appreciated you for all the *little* things you did? Be that rare person who recognizes people for these things.

Resources

http://www.huffingtonpost.com/mequilibrium/gratitude-benefits_b_3321351.html

http://www.huffingtonpost.com/2014/07/21/gratitude-healthy-benefits_n_2147182.html

Habit 5 – Morning Productivity

Remembering that momentum generates motivation, how can you generate momentum that carries over to everything else you do over the course of the day?

The habit I've find highly effective for this is using the first 20 – 60 minutes of my morning to be proactive rather than reactive. What that means is instead of my old habit of checking emails and Facebook and responding to whatever I saw, I'd use that time to work on an important project.

While writing this book, this meant writing a chapter before doing anything else which set a tone for the entire day. I now feel productive right from the start of the day, and I want to keep knocking things off my to-do list. I also feel more confident throughout the day because I know I've accomplished something.

I suggest setting aside a few minutes first thing in the morning to do something that will move your life forward. You can obviously combine this with any of your other habits such as exercise, gratitude, or reading. Also, while doing something like reading personal development is a highly recommended habit, I suggest using at least part of this time to *apply* the things you're learning. This takes you from a mere *consumer* of information to an *applier* of information.

This can be a flexible habit. That means what I do to be productive one morning might be writing, and then another morning might be recording a video. The important thing is I think of one or two high priority tasks I can complete that are in alignment with my goals.

Suggested Micro-Habit
Take two minutes to work on something productive.

Suggested Upgrade
Create a 20 – 60 minute morning routine that will either be dedicated to a single project, or use this as a "healthy habit time" that stacks a combination of exercise, reading, meditation, and whatever other good habits you'd like to knock out first thing in the morning.

Example of a 60 minute healthy habit stack: 10 minutes meditating. 20 minutes working on a project. 5 minutes doing light exercise asking yourself what you're grateful for. 20 minutes intense exercise. 5 minute cool-down while considering how you can be even better today than yesterday.

Resources
Eat That Frog by Brian Tracy
Habit Stacking by S.J. Scott
Wake Up Successful by S.J. Scott

Bonus: "5 Reasons People Fail With Mini Habits" by Stephen Guise

Derek's note: The book Mini Habits by Stephen Guise is something I consider a bit of a must-read for people that join my online challenge groups. That's because Stephen does such an excellent job at breaking down the power and practical application of, what I call, a micro-habit. While the concept is simple, in coaching others, I've found some people still manage to screw it up. Check out Stephen's advice on how to avoid these common mistakes.

The Mini Habits strategy has been successful for a great majority of people who've tried it. I've lost count of the success stories, and as of writing, it's the highest-rated habit book amongst top sellers at 4.7 stars. The high success rate can be attributed to the core idea that a mini habit should be small enough to complete even on your worst day. If you can complete your goals on your worst day, what can stop you? Not much!

But as with any strategy, there are exceptions. I've paid very close attention to anyone who has said, "this didn't work for me." Here are the top five reasons people fail with Mini Habits, based on cases of people who have not succeeded.

1. Forgetting & Not Taking Their Mini Habit(s) Seriously

To succeed with mini habits, you must treat them with respect. This isn't an issue with any other goal, because larger goals demand respect naturally. Visiting Greece—something I want to do—is a significant and noteworthy action that automatically earns my respect. A mini habit of one push-up seems worthless at first glance.

A key focus of the Mini Habits book is to show you why doing something like 1+ push-up per day is surprisingly powerful when done consistently. If the book succeeds in delivering this message, the reader succeeds. But if that message is lost and the mini habit is seen as unimportant, you will probably "forget to do it."

Forgetting to do a mini habit every once in a while isn't a big deal. I've forgotten to read 5 times in 10 months and I've never forgotten to write. That's because writing is more important to me right now than reading is. But I've still read much more because of my reading mini habit.

Generally speaking, if you're forgetting once a week or more, you're not taking it seriously.

Would you forget to do your third day of an intense program like P90X? Of course not, because it's too big to ignore. You might purposefully choose not to do it because it's too hard, but you wouldn't likely completely forget about it.

Forgetting something is often a sign that it's unimportant to you (I don't remember what I ate for breakfast last Tuesday). Some people just forget easily, however, and if this is you, then you can set up reminders or adopt a time or action-based cue.

Mini habits work best for people who are eager to change themselves, and their habits, permanently. If you have this mindset going in, you'll take your easy daily commitment seriously, and you will change your life. If you treat your mini habit(s) like an afterthought, then it's possible you're not interested to change that area or else you don't understand the power of consistency.

2. Setting Too Many Mini Habits

One reader was so excited with his early success that he started ten mini habits. I warned him. It resulted in him only doing the minimum for each one, feeling burdened, and not feeling very successful. The last I heard from him, he trimmed down to 5 mini habits and was doing well with them.

Having a lot of mini habits seems possible because they're so small. But you must put their small size in the perspective of **doing them every single day**. Reading two pages in a book is nothing, but doing it every day does require some extra effort and commitment.

I think each extra mini habit you add is more exponential than additional. The difference between three and four mini habits is more than you'd think! I still seem to do best with three mini habits.

If you stick to the recommended 1-4 mini habits and adjust to your situation, you should do fine, but if you take on more than four at a time and it doesn't work, you can't blame the system, because you're not following the system. Don't be in such a rush to change, because your brain will only change slowly, even if you "want it."

3. Not Wanting The Habit

Mini habits work best when you truly want the habit and lifestyle change, be it writing, reading, exercise, gardening, cooking, or developing your public speaking skills. If you attempt to change yourself because someone expects you to change or because it seems like you "should eat better," you have a great chance to fail.

No strategy can overcome a divided self.

4. Too Small Of A Start

In the beginning, I said no step is too small. I have revised that.

When a reader told me she had written 30 words in 30 days, I immediately understood why her goal was too small. "A" is a word, "the" is a word, and alone, these words aren't meaningful. You can write them mindlessly and without *any* effort.

A good mini habit starts you off with some momentum. One push-up is an excellent boost to a hesitant exerciser. It requires a sliver of effort, and it gets you on the ground in position, where you can easily do more. Writing 50 words has been an excellent boost to my writing, because it's very easy, yet requires me to get thinking about what I want to write about.

Reading 2 pages has been on/off successful for me. About 30% of the time, I only read the two pages. But sometimes I get hooked and read a lot more. I find it depends on the book! One book I'm reading now is *Thinking: Fast and Slow* by Daniel Kahneman, and its density requires a lot of thought and processing, so I'm moving through it slower. I also find it a little bit less interesting than the last book I read: *The Willpower Instinct*.

The perfect mini habit is too easy to say no to, and yet it will be big enough to bring you meaningful forward momentum in the direction you desire.

5. Secret Goals

The last one in our list is one that all people who implement mini habits will struggle with at some level at some point in time. It's tempting to expect more from yourself than your mini habit, but it undermines the low bar we're trying to set. The idea that you mini habit goal *is enough* can be difficult to accept because we want to do more and be more.

Keep this advice in mind: be satisfied with your minimum, and eager to overachieve.

The fundamentally different approach of mini habits is getting your small win, and then giving yourself freedom. The benefits of autonomy (i.e. having freedom to make meaningful decisions) have been shown to give an impressive boost to intrinsic motivation, and the mini habits concept is the only concept I know of that has autonomy built into it.

Whereas most strategies are guilt- or pressure-driven, mini habits take the pressure off, empower you, and then let you decide how much extra, if any, you would like to do. So be wary of giving yourself bigger goals, and remember that small goals don't hold you back—they only ensure that you start.

This concept turned me from a lazy, unproductive writer into a fit, writing machine. Two days ago, I discovered that I can now grab the rim on a 10 ft basketball goal (I'm 5'11"). My path to this level of fitness (which continues to improve further) started with one push-up, which is why I know anyone can succeed with mini habits!

About Stephen: Stephen Guise is the author of the acclaimed, best-selling book, Mini Habits, and creator of the popular Mini Habit Mastery Video Course In 2011, shortly after realizing he wasn't a 9-to-5 kind of guy, Stephen founded the Deep Existence blog, which helps people change their behavior primarily through unorthodox, yet highly effective habit modification and focusing strategies. His Finance degree remains unused as he enjoys the greater freedom and satisfaction that comes from helping people live better lives.

Bonus: "The Hawthorne Effect: How Observation Helps You Maintain A Habit Change" by S.J. Scott

Derek's notes: S.J. Scott is a prolific writer on the topic of developing better habits. His blog http://developgoodhabits.com is filled with tips, tricks, and ideas for improving your habits. It's also a great resource when you're looking for ideas on actual habits you'd like to work on. In this article, he discusses what I consider to be the #1 motivator to have in place when you want to make a big shift in your life – accountability. The following article is from his blog and can be found here: http://www.developgoodhabits.com/hawthorne-effect/

Developing a habit isn't always as easy as it sounds.

In fact, you often need as much help as possible to follow through.

One possible solution is to use a classic psychological principle to your advantage.

Specially, there's a study called the **Hawthorne Effect** (or *Observer Effect*) which has been proven to improve performance in the completion of tasks.

In this article, we'll talk about the Hawthorne Effect and how you can use it to reinforce good habits and eliminate bad habits.

Let's get to it.

What is the Hawthorne Effect?

The term *Hawthorne Effect* was coined in the 1950's based on a series of experiments that were originally conducted in the 1920's.

In an industrial experiment which was conducted to see whether factory workers were more productive with a greater or lesser amount of ambient lighting, researchers found that productivity of BOTH groups increased from the control amounts.

After further experiments it became clear that this result happened *because* the test subjects knew they were being studied.

The lesson learned?

When people are being observed they want to look good and perform well.

It is human nature. If we know we're being watched, it's natural to increase our performance and give that little bit of extra effort.

The Hawthorne Effect and YOU.

How does this information help you form positive habits?

Well, if you've read other posts on DevelopGoodHabits.com, then you know that **accountability** is a critical part of habit development. Whether you've trying to change a bad habit or reinforce a good one (*like the building a writing routine and walking 10,000 steps a day*), having accountability is an essential part of making it happen.

The Hawthorne Effect shows that we do better when we know we're being watched and reviewed by others. So to improve your chances of success all you have to do is put yourself out there to *be observed* by others.

How to Implement The Hawthorne Effect

Saying, "put yourself out there" is simple enough, but you might wonder how to do it. So let's go over five ways you use the Hawthorne Effect to your advantage:

#1: Family and Friends. Tell those closest to you and you'll get moral support from the people who love you most.

#2: Social Media. Twitter, Facebook or Google+ provide you with a powerful platform to stay on top of your habit change. Simply promise you'll post the results every day and you'll get motivational messages to follow through.

#3: Accountability Partners and Mastermind Groups. One of the reasons all the "Anonymous" groups are successful is because of the Hawthorne Effect. Finding someone, or a group, who are trying to reach the same goal gives you a place to discuss problems and overcome obstacles. Ultimately these people will help you avoid backsliding into a negative routine.

#4: Habit-Specific Tools and Apps. Nowadays, there are a wide range of tools, software and apps that help you stay on top of a goal. Not only do they track your performance, they also provide an opportunity to "compete" with your friends on the achievement of a goal.

For instance, not only does the FitBit count your daily steps, it also syncs with Facebook where you can measure the results against your peers. You better believe this helps you stay motivated during those rainy days when you don't feel like exercising.

#5: Blog. Blogs are cheap and easy to make. WordPress and Blogger are just two of the 100% free options to get started with blogging. If you are starting a diet, quitting smoking, creating an exercise routine or trying any other habit change, you can share your experiences with the world.

Blogging is beneficial because it provides a place for coalescing your thoughts and thinking through any challenges you're currently experiencing. In reality, not many people will read it, but you'll still feel accountable because you know someone *might* stumble across it.

3 Steps for Getting Started with the Hawthorne Effect

It's not hard to implement the Hawthorne Effect.

In fact, you can break it down into three easy steps:

Identify a habit you'd like to develop (here are 203 ideas.)

Focus on this new routine for the next 30 days.

Add *public accountability* so people expect you to follow through.

Simple, right?

Since you now know that your performance improves when you're being observed, it only makes sense to purposefully add some form of public disclosure to every habit you develop.

Now it's time to take action.

Follow these three steps for your next habit change and you'll increase your chances of success.

About S.J. Scott: Steve Scott believes in the idea of developing one habit at a time, which is the core philosophy of his blog Develop Good Habits. In addition to experimenting with different habits every month, he writes about his experiences in short, actionable Kindle books, which can be found at HabitBooks.com. When not working, S.J. likes to read, exercise and explore the different parts of the world.t

Bonus: "Developing Habits: The Variable of the Equation You've Been Missing" by Jimmie Brenton

Derek's note: Jimmie shares a great strategy for not only developing better habits by making them easier, but also overcoming poor habits by making them more difficult. When I wanted to cut down on Facebook time, I used a similar strategy by telling myself I could only check Facebook if I made a post or comment. This made the task harder to do mindlessly and forced me to be consciously aware of my behavior.

You're ready to change your habits. You've rearranged your schedule, you've bought any items you need and you're mentally charged and excited for what the future will bring. You've done everything right. So why is it that time after time new habits fail to stick around while our old habits, like a snake, slither back into our lives?

What did I do wrong?

Didn't I do everything I was supposed to?

Do I just not have the willpower to succeed?

Have you ever asked yourself any of those questions before? For many of us, the steps we think we need to take in order to succeed aren't enough. We often spend too much time focusing on the building of a new habit and its future benefits, and not enough time focusing on the old habit itself. This is also why the *New York Times* reported that 80% of us break our New Year's resolutions within the first month. (1) Do 80% of us unconsciously not want to succeed?

The answer is not that we don't want to succeed, the answer is that we're still missing a pivotal variable in our equation for success.

I believe author Shawn Achor describes it best in his book *The Happiness Advantage: The Seven Principles of Positive Psychology That Fuel Success and Performance at Work*. Achor states, "lower the activation energy for habits you want to adopt, and raise it for the habits you want to avoid." (2) To make his idea even more simple let us break it down into the following equation:

easier NEW HABIT
+ harder OLD HABIT
SUCCESSFUL CHANGE

You see, too often we spend 100% of our time focusing on the new habit, and all of its future benefits, that we neglect the second half of the equation; making the old habit more difficult. However, it is the second half of the equation where the real change takes place.

Let's look at an all too common example of someone wanting to lose weight and eat healthier. We'll call this person Sandy. Sandy, like many, has trouble staying away from snacks and other unhealthy foods that fill up her refrigerator and pantry. No matter how hard she tries, no matter how much she diets, no matter how many meal plans she tries to follow, the same foods make their way back into her life time after time.

Together, let's help Sandy make this new habit (eating healthier) easier. Instead Sandy is now going to keep healthy snacks closer at hand. She is going to make sure she has simple and constant access to fruits and veggies instead of only cookies and crackers. To make it even easier, Sandy is going to keep the new healthy snacks physically closer than the unhealthy snacks, like in a bowl that she has to walk by before reaching the refrigerator or pantry.

Sandy has now completed step one. She has made the new habit easier than the old one. This is where most people stop, and for some perhaps this is enough. But since you now know the missing variable to this equation you know we're only half way there.

Let us solidify this new habit for Sandy. We need to make those snacks even tougher for Sandy to get to (making the old habit harder) on the days where her willpower dwindles and temptation takes over. One possibility would be to take the unhealthy snacks and place them in the back of the refrigerator (behind the healthy options) or high up in the pantry a foot stool away from reach.

Even more ironclad for Sandy is to simply stop buying the unhealthy snacks and treats. The age old out of sight, out of mind method. Now when Sandy is at home and a craving kicks in she will have to leave her home, get in her car, drive to the store, buy the item and then drive home to enjoy a treat. That's a lot of work that most likely no one will would be willing to do.

Either way we have made the new habit (eating healthier) easier by making healthy options easier for her to grab and we've made the old habit (unhealthy snacking) more difficult by making the snacks either hard to reach or by not even buying them. We've fulfilled both parts of the equation increasing drastically Sandy's success.

Conclusion

What habits have you tried to change in the past that haven't stuck? Did you think to make the old habit more difficult on yourself?

The answer to creating new habits may not always be easy to see. In many cases you may even have to get quite creative in your brainstorming process. I have heard of people removing batteries from the TV remote, placing locks on cabinets, wearing workout clothing to bed and more. The point is no matter what habits you're trying to adopt make sure you follow the equation for success to make those habits truly stick. Remember the formula is simple...

easier NEW HABIT
+ harder OLD HABIT
SUCCESSFUL CHANGE

Adopting Your Own Habits

Now it is time to apply this formula to your own life. For some, the answers will jump out at you and you will begin forming new habits instantly. For others ask yourself these questions to help guide your process.

Ask yourself…

Are you creatively making the new habits fit as easily into your lifestyle as possible?

Is there a way to make these new habits even easier on yourself? Ask a friend for help too!

Are you creatively making the old bad habits more difficult for yourself?

Is there a way to make these old habits even more difficult on yourself? It's ok to be a bit extreme here. Again, ask a friend for more help.

Parker-Pope, T. (December 13, 2007). Will your resolutions last until February? New York Times. Citing a study by Franklin Covey of 15,000 people.

2 Achor, Shawn. (2010). The Happiness Advantage: Seven Principles of Positive Psychology That Fuel Success and Performance at Work. New York, Crown Business. p161.

About Jimmie Brenton: Jimmie Brenton believes that everyone has the power to design their own life, which is the driving force behind his blog Live by DESIGN. Having been stuck and afraid to take action for much of his own life Jimmie now studies and helps others learn what it takes to take action and improve their own lives.

You can find more information at www.JimmieBrenton.com and make sure to follow along for his upcoming book releasing in 2015. When not working Jimmie likes to challenge himself with extreme fitness sports, creating graphic art and traveling.

Bonus: Matt Stone on Intrinsic Motivation

Derek's note: Matt brings up a great point that I briefly touch on when picking a healthy habit – start with something you find relatively enjoyable. When I got into exercise, I didn't work on the habit of running on a treadmill. I started with weight lifting because I found it more entertaining and it had more perceived benefits. Eventually, my passion for other forms of exercise grew. The greatest accomplishments in my life have come from following a passion while still being willing to step out of my comfort zone.

A contribution from me in a book about habits is almost criminally hypocritical. The only thing I do habitually is complain! Kidding.

However, over the past eight years, I'm known for having achieved great feats of productivity. I've started several businesses, written several *million* words, read 400 books, helped publish over 100, and so on. In my 20s, before I embarked on a mission to use my brain so productively, I walked more than 10,000 miles! Yet I've managed to do this without any habits at all.

Now, I've got nothing against habits. Truth be told, my day-to-day life could use quite a tune-up. I need more exercise. I need more sleep. Making a wholesome breakfast this morning instead of impulsively driving to the nearest doughnut shop at 11am wouldn't have hurt. I struggle to form good habits in these areas. Yet, I'm insanely productive elsewhere. What gives?

I want to let you in on a little secret. It's common sense really, but if you don't stop to think carefully about it, you might miss it. So here goes...

If you're doing what you want to do, you don't need to do a lot of work on your habits, you don't need goals—you don't need any outside motivation to help keep you on track. If you are in the throes of passion, you experience *intrinsic* motivation to do it, which is a wellspring of energy and enthusiasm that doesn't require a kick in the pants to pursue.

The problem I always used to run into is when I tried to form habits and set goals to do something I really didn't want to do. That's why I tried so hard to coerce myself to do it. It's also why I failed. Try as I might, attempts to force myself to do something I didn't like expired quickly. And I almost always set goals and attempted to forge habits in areas that I didn't have a natural affinity for. Not only did I spend a lot of time forcing myself to do unwanted tasks, but I also spent a lot of time cursing myself for my lack of "discipline" and "willpower." Experiencing repeated bouts of intensifying self-directed guilt and disappointment took its toll. I felt like I was at war with myself most of the time.

But at 27 something magical happened. I attended a seminar that was about identifying your true passions—those areas where intrinsic motivation freely flowed. I realized that, without any coercion whatsoever, I was actually being quite productive. In the seminar we were encouraged to stop doing what we didn't want to do and start spending as much of our time as possible doing what we liked doing instead. What a concept!

Not only did my life improve dramatically when I started spending a lot more time doing things I loved and a lot less time doing things I didn't, but my productivity ran off the charts, and I quickly began building skills, abilities, knowledge, and expertise in ways I never have been able to before.

For example, I always hated reading. I mean *really* hated reading. I had tried to read books in the past, but I rarely finished them. The problem?

I was reading books about things I wasn't interested in. The solution? I started reading books about what I was most interested in. I began to read more than 50 books per year (more than I had read in my first 27 years total), and because they were always about exactly what I was most interested in at any given moment, my retention of the subject matter was unlike anything I'd ever experienced.

Within five years I had become a respected authority and scholar in my area of interest (even though I was a mediocre student all my life), I was making a full-time income from it, and I was not just happy but *fulfilled*, which I think is a far more powerful sensation than happiness.

In short, the idea is that we make it farther in life, faster—and enjoy our lives more to boot—when we are spending our time doing what we love rather than doing what we hate. Simple enough, but quite powerful for those that need to hear it.

Take this concept with you when thinking about what habits you want to form. If you try to form habits to do things you don't like, it will be an uphill battle. If it feels easy, if it feels intuitive, and if you become increasingly eager to do what you've set out to do more of (read, write, exercise, clean, study, etc.) as you continue—then you've probably found something that is authentically YOU. Don't stop!

Achieve greatness doing what you love, and then pay someone to do all the things you hate doing once you have. That's exactly what I'm doing, and I've delegated so much of my workload at this point that I finally have the time to start hitting the trail again.

Matt Stone is the author of way too many books under way too many pen names, founder of www.180degreehealth.com and www.buckbooks.net, and co-founder of www.archangelink.com. For more on enhancing your productivity without doing stuff you don't like doing, read Goals Suck: Why the Obsession with Goal-Setting is a Flawed Approach to Productivity and Life in General.

Bonus: "The Psychological Woes Of Physique Enhancement" by JC Deen

Derek's note: JC Deen of jcdfitness.com is a fitness coach who excels at helping people overcome the mental barriers to staying fit. In this excerpt from one of his blog posts, he reveals a few of the psychological pitfalls that sabotage many people's fitness success. If you want to discover and resolve even more of these pitfalls, I highly suggest his book Stay Leaner Longer.

The Negative Feedback Loop

Let's consider a typical scenario for someone who doesn't get the results they want. All this is hypothetical, but is happening right now for many people.

We'll use 'he' in the case of Joe, but it's happening to women as well.

He started out training with the goal of looking better.

After a few weeks in the gym, he's not seeing the results he wants. That night he goes on the internet and researches the best workout for **ripped abs**, and a million search results come up.

4 hours later, and a lot of reading, he decides on a new plan. He's excited, and ready for results.

The next day he starts the routine, and does it for the next week.

Turns out the program is really challenging. He realizes he can't dedicate 6 days to training, and he missed his morning workouts over the weekend.

During the following week, he feels bad for missing the workouts, and stares at himself in the mirror. He sees a weak physique and decides the program is not working, and begins his search for a new one.

While he's searching, he comes across a diet that seems to make losing fat a breeze. Effortless, even.

He begins following that.

The first week is hard, but he is determined.

According to the new diet protocol, carbs make you fat.

So he eliminates all starch, eats nothing but lean meat, leafy greens, and limits carb intake to 25g of dextrose in his post-workout shake.

At the end of the week, he's asked to attend a birthday party on Saturday night, but refuses so he's not tempted to eat any 'bad foods.'

Sunday morning, he wakes up ravenous due to slashing his calorie intake in half the week before, and proceeds to eat everything in the house.

He tries to avoid the temptation, but cravings are out of control.

That night he decided to call this his 'refeed' so as to make himself feel a little better.

After some reflection, he learns that choosing to miss out on a social event due to his 'diet' restrictions made him a little depressed.

He wakes up 10 pounds heavier from the drastic intake of carbs, glycogen refilling into his muscles, and of course holding tons of water.

He hates the bloat he's sporting in the mirror and even calls himself a failure under his breath.

In his head, he tells himself he'll never change. After some more sulking, he heads back to the internet for another magic bullet.

He finds it, and proceeds to repeat the above scenario over and over again the coming months.

Eventually, he'll look back and say "I've been training and dieting for years—nothing works for me!"

For many people who claim that nothing works, a similar pattern is at play.

An inability to practice consistency coupled with unrealistic expectations is a surefire way to feeling bad about yourself.

When you feel bad about yourself, you try to cope.

Why We Fail

When we act on emotions, as opposed to logic and rationality, we often make bad decisions.

Joe, in the example above, always deferred to his emotions and how he felt he was progressing, or how he felt a diet was working, **as opposed to what was really going on.**

His actions were never grounded in a foundation of hard work, consistency, and effort. He acted on a whim, making changes when he was emotional.

You can only control what you track, and measure, over the weeks, months, and years, not an hourly or daily basis.

We fail when we give into the shortcut mentality. We fail when we think the results are easy to achieve.

We fail when we get into the negative feedback loops full of negative self-talk and sabotage.

Don't be like Joe. Choose your goal, develop realistic expectations, track your progress, and get the support or accountability when you need it.

See full article at: http://www.jcdfitness.com/2014/05/the-psychological-woes-of-physique-enhancement/

About JC Deen: JC Deen is a fitness coach, writer, and owner of JCD Fitness, based in Nashville, Tennessee. He's been published in Men's Health, TNATION, Men's Fitness, Forbes online, and Bodybuilding.com. JC works with clients who want more strength, mobility and aesthetic improvements. He is the creator of the complete fitness solution LGN365 and author of the book Stay Leaner Longer. Visit his website www.jcdfitness.com for more from him.

Bonus: "The Psychology Behind Habit Formation" by Maneesh Sethi & The Pavlok Team

Derek's notes: Maneesh is an expert on habit development and is leading the development of the groundbreaking Pavlok device which helps train you to create better habits using advanced technology.

The Three-Step Process to Form Habits

Habits range in complexity. Some are simple, while others are complex. Putting on one shoe before the other -- simple. Grocery shopping -- complex. You need to drive to the grocery store, get out of your car and walk in, go over to the aisle where you'll find what you need, then go to another aisle, walk to the checkout lines, wait for the line to move forward, grab the Snickers bar while waiting for the cashier to check you out, walk back to the car, drive home. Complex habits are actually just a combination of several smaller habits that are being performed in succession.

The first part of how to form habits is the cue. This is a trigger that tells your brain, "Okay -- time to do X." Once that happens, the brain starts performing the behavior without any conscious effort on your part. So when you walk to the checkout counter, your hand will automatically reach for the Snickers bar without a second thought. That's just what it is used to doing, and has been doing it for a long time. The first time you did it, it was a conscious decision. After that, not so much. After the first time, the brain doesn't even think about what is happening. The habit is triggered automatically.

The actual act of buying and eating the Snickers bar is called the routine. The routine isn't necessarily physical though. Watching a guy drive past in a Ferrari could be a trigger for you to have self-doubts about your success in life. Habits are anything that you do without conscious thought. They happen without you deciding to make them happen.

Finally, there is the reward. This is what the brain and body get for going through the routine. The pleasure of enjoying the Snickers bar reinforces the behavior. The more often the brain uses this process, the deeper the behavior becomes ingrained. Eventually, the cue will trigger a craving for the reward, leading to action.

This process of habit formation oftentimes occurs unintentionally, without a conscious decision. As long as there is a consistent cue and a pleasurable reward, you'll form a habit. This leads to us developing habits that we don't really want.

Fortunately, we can use this process to our benefit. We can identify habits that are desirable, and use the cue-routine-reward process to ingrain them into our everyday lives.

Moreover, we can use this process to change habits. It is very hard to destroy habits. Instead, they should be replaced. And the best way to replace habits is to keep the same cue and reward, and replace the routine. By doing so, you are consciously filling the void left by erasing a bad habit and adding a better one in its place. Instead of eating ice cream you have a bowl of frozen berries, fulfilling the desire for a cold treat without the caloric load and other effects of having ice cream.

In summary, the cue-routine-reward is the three-step process in which habits are formed, either consciously or unconsciously, whether you're replacing a habit or forming a new one.

Why Willpower and Motivation Aren't Enough

Think about the last time you failed when trying to form a new habit. Did you blame failure on willpower? Do you think you need more willpower to be successful?

If so, you've got it partly wrong.

Yes, willpower is important. Clearly we need willpower to follow the courses of action we set for ourselves. Yet, willpower alone is not sufficient to get us to form those habits. According to psychologist Roy Baumeister, willpower is like a muscle (see an excellent summary of his most recent book here). It can be depleted from doing tasks that require the control of impulses.

This is why habits can't be formed from brute force alone. You'll fail if your method relies on your willpower alone. You're human, and sooner or later, you'll have a day where you're feeling tired and lacking in energy.

The same goes for motivation -- it also is important, but definitely not enough.

You need to have a reason for your habit change, but more importantly, you need to keep that reason in mind. Not just the cue, and reward, but the big-picture goal that you can receive from having changed your habit. However, motivation will not get you out of bed at 5 in the morning so that you can meditate, neither will willpower. What will help you is mindset and systems. You need to have developed a proper framework to deal with these situations.

About Maneesh: Maneesh Sethi is the Founder and CEO of Pavlok - The Wearable Wristband That Trains Your Habits With Electric Shock. He was the keynote speaker to London's Royal Society of Medicine and has written 4 books, including an international bestseller. After studying at Stanford University with habit professor BJ Fogg, Maneesh started multiple companies while traveling the world and helped launch numerous New York Times bestsellers including The 4-Hour Chef by Tim Ferriss. Find out about him and his wearable habit-training device at http://pavlok.com/

Bonus: "Saying No" by Tom Corson-Knowles

Derek's note: The following is from Tom Corson-Knowle's productivity book Destroy Your Distractions. He explains why saying "no" is essential to creating space for better habits in your life. Tom is a personal mentor of mine who has taught me quite a bit about what it takes to be successful as an entrepreneur, and many of his insights apply to anyone wanting to find more success, happiness, and productivity. I highly recommend checking out his other books which span a variety of topics on his author page: http://www.amazon.com/Tom-Corson-Knowles/e/B008QHU66C

Whenever someone asks for your time, saying no should be your default response. The biggest missed opportunities are the ones right in front of you that you get distracted from completing. Hoping a random opportunity will make you rich is like trying to win the lottery. The odds are never in your favor, and you just might go broke trying to get there.

Everyone who has achieved a high level of success in any area of life has done so by saying no to distractions. We all must say no more than we say yes. By choosing to get married and be loyal to your spouse, you must say no to all the other potential partners. That's a few billion no's for one yes.

Likewise, when you say yes and commit to a business venture or opportunity, you must say no to others so that you can focus on what's most important to you. Saying no isn't about being rude or mean or disinterested in others. Instead, it's about being focused on what's most important to you. You don't need to apologize to anyone for doing the right thing, whether that's staying loyal to your spouse or staying committed to your most important work in life.

If you really want to be successful, focus on your own priorities, not other peoples' priorities. Live your own life, not someone else's. You may feel bad for turning people down and saying no but it will allow you to say yes to what's most important to you. And if something is most important to you it means that everything else is less important. Don't let unimportant things stop you from achieving what is most important to you.

SIMPLICITY

Live a simpler life, not a simple life. Understand the 80/20 rule. The 80/20 rule says that 80% of your success will come from 20% of what you do. The 20% is comprised of the most important people, things and work in your life. The 80% is everything else. It's not that the 80% is bad – it's just not what's most important and impactful in your life right now.

Learn to focus on the 20% - the few people, places, and things that are most important to you. Everything else may come and go, but these few people and things will remain the foundation of your life.

At least 80% of what you own could be thrown out and it would not materially affect your happiness. You will want to get rid of at least 80% of your ideas. It's the 20% or less that's left that you want to keep, nourish and grow. I'm not saying you should go throw out 80% of your possessions right now. I'm just encouraging you to focus on what's most important to you, so you can be grateful for it and get what you really want out of life.

Whenever you feel pulled trying to please everyone, or keep everything you own, or do everything you could do, remember to focus on what's most important. Be willing to let everything else go if it means you'll keep hold of what's most important to you.

About Tom: Tom Corson-Knowles is the international best-selling author of more than twenty books including The Kindle Publishing Bible and is the founder of TCK Publishing, an independent publishing company specializing in digital marketing. He teaches authors how to turn their writing into a profitable career at www. EbookPublishingSchool.com. You can connect with Tom on Twitter and Facebook.

Bonus: "20 Mile March" by James Roper and Chandler Bolt

Derek's notes: The following is an excerpt from the highly recommended book The Productive Person by James Roper and Chandler Bolt. You'll notice something many high achievers have in common — consistency. The process of breaking down a habit into micro-habits is much like process of breaking down big goals into smaller daily actions.

If you've read "Great by Choice" by Jim Collins, you've heard of the 20-Mile March concept; if not, we'll explain it for you.

The story starts with 2 teams of adventurers both trying to become the first people to reach the South Pole. They had the same equipment and skills, but very different strategies. The strategy of the first team was to complete a 20-mile march daily, no matter the weather.

The other team would push themselves on days with good weather, sometimes hiking 40-60 miles in a single day. But when the weather was bad, they would hunker down and go nowhere. The team with the 20-mile march made it to the South Pole first and returned alive while the other team died trying.

To find your own 20-Mile March, you need to figure out your end goal and the action steps needed to get there.

Once you've figured out what action steps you will be taking, there are a couple of ways you can build them into your daily routine as habits: a physical calendar or a check-in counting app. Both do the same thing; it's just a matter of preference.

Comedian Jerry Seinfeld created the calendar approach that is referred to as "Don't break the chain." When he decided he wanted to be a comedian, he committed to writing 1 joke every single day. He printed off a calendar of the entire year and taped it to his wall. Every day when he wrote a joke, he would put an X through that day. He continued writing jokes every day so that he wouldn't break the chain of X's.

Another example of a 20-Mile March comes from someone who committed to writing 1,000 words a day for an entire year. Within that year, he wrote 2 best-selling books and launched a successful info product. He made over $ 250,000 that year, up from the $ 60,000 he made the year before.

The 20-Mile March uses the power of streaks. It's these streaks that force you to keep moving forward, even when you're having an off day. Don't believe me?? Try it. Get to a 30-day streak and see if you don't jump out of bed and hit the floor at 11 o'clock at night when you remember you haven't done your 100 push-ups.

Having a good Accountabilibuddy to complete these exercises with is one of the greatest ways to see sustained results and change. These are the exact exercises we use and teach to college students to enable them to start and run businesses that generate hundreds of thousands of dollars each year. It works for them, and it can work for you too ... as long as you have a good Accountabilibuddy.

Choose wisely who you work with, because without them, this schedule will not work. If you're always keeping them accountable but they're not reciprocating, find a new Accountabilibuddy!

Even with the best Accountabilibuddy, all of us occasionally find ourselves off course. The next schedule can be planned, but sometimes it just happens. Regardless of how you find yourself needing to work into the night, we'll show you how to flip the switch in the afternoon and make the second half of your day productive.

About James and Chandler: James and Chandler are the authors of the #1 bestselling book The Productive Person. You can get a free audiobook edition of the book by going here: http://www.theproductiveperson.com.

Resources: Recommended Websites

In no particular order of significance:

ExcuseProof.com – My personal website where I share tips and tricks to stay fit on a busy schedule, with a limited budget, and when completely lacking motivation.

UpgradeYourHabits.com/challenge – Sign-up for my free online challenge groups here.

ZenHabits.net – One of the best sites for simple, practical tips to develop better habits, simplify your life, and increase your productivity. I especially love Leo's take on goals and meditation.

JCDFitness.com – Run by JC Deen, this a great site if you want workout plans and diet suggestions for getting fit. JC also covers many of the psychological pitfalls people encounter on their journey to improving their bodies.

JamesClear.com – James is a leading authority on habit development. I highly suggest checking out his newsletter which is filled with awesome articles on the psychology of habits.

ComfortPit.com – Jon provides tons of tips for improving your life, and the best part is he's strict about making sure they have scientific backing. There are a lot of other interesting articles there on things like lucid dreaming, speed reading that actually works, and the benefits of meditation.

HackTheSystem.com – Hack the System is run by Maneesh Sethi. He shares general life hacks for things like productivity, fitness, making money, and more.

Pavlok.com – Pavlok is a cutting-edge technology designed to help you break bad habits and develop better habits.

DevelopGoodHabits.com – Run by bestselling author SJ Scott, this blog is filled with ideas for better habits, 30 day habit challenge guides, and guest articles from leading authorities on self-improvement.

StevePavlina.com – Steve runs one of the most famous personal development blogs on the internet. If it's related to improving your life, he probably touches on it.

ScottHYoung.com – Scott has a great series on developing habits as well as improving your learning. He has quite a bit of scientific backing behind his information, and he breaks it down in an easy to understand way.

TinyHabits.com and BJFogg.com – The two websites run by BJ Fogg who is, as far as I know, the original person to popularize the concept of what I refer to as micro-habits.

PsyBlog.co.uk - Psychologist Dr. Jeremy Dean breaks down the latest psychological research into incredible entertaining and practical reads. A great site for those who like practical application of cutting-edge research and want to be entertained at the same time.

Stickk.com – A resource to create accountability for yourself online. Allows you to put money on the line to donate to charity if you don't follow through a goal.

Resources: Recommended Habit Books

Mini Habits by Stephen Guise

The Power of Habit by Charles Duhigg

Habit Stacking by S.J. Scott

Bad Habits No More by S.J. Scott

Resolutions That Stick by S.J. Scott

The Compound Effect by Darren Hardy

Transform Your Habits by James Clear

Habit Change Theory and Practice by Maneesh Sethi and The Pavlok Team

Productivity Habit Related

The Productive Person by James Roper and Chandler Bolt

Destroy Your Distractions by Tom Corson-Knowles

Getting Things Done by David Allen

Stress Habit Related

Doc Orman's Books

Fitness Habit Related

Weight Loss Motivation Hacks by Derek Doepker

50 Fitness Tips You Wish You Knew by Derek Doepker

Stay Leaner Longer by JC Deen

Happiness and Success Habit Related

Why You're Stuck by Derek Doepker

7 Habits of Highly Successful People by Stephen R. Covey

Resources: Recommended Habit Articles

Struggling With Your Habits? Three Questions You Need To Ask Yourself: http://www.developgoodhabits.com/three-questions - Article by me on the three questions you can ask yourself to stick to your better habits when you're finding it challenging. I reveal one of my most powerful questions to unleashing motivation.

30 Challenges For 30 Days: http://www.highexistence.com/30-challenges-for-30-days - Full of great micro-habit ideas and their difficulty rating. This article is great to brainstorm healthy habits to incorporate into your life.

How To Design The Perfect Morning Routine: http://www.highexistence.com/how-to-design-the-perfect-morning-routine - This article from Jon Brooks of ComfortPit.com is one of the best I've seen on designing a daily routine. It shows you how to balance structure with flexibility.

This Coach Improved Every Tiny Thing by 1 Percent and Here's What Happened: http://jamesclear.com/marginal-gains - This article from James Clear will open your eyes to the compounding effect of tiny improvements over the long-haul.

Successful People Start Before They Feel Ready: http://jamesclear. com/successful-people-start-before-they-feel-ready - A key concept in this book is that you act before you have full insight into the journey ahead of you. James Clear lays out this concept with some incredible real-world examples from Sir Richard Branson.

What Strengthens and Weakens Our Integrity – Part I: Why Small Choices Count: http://www.artofmanliness.com/2013/08/05/what-strengthens-and-weakens-our-integrity-part-i-why-small-choices-count - The article series that really opened my eyes to the impact of small choices. It also was my first introduction to the "what the hell" effect.

Fitness Related Articles

Forming Habits, How I Do It, and Why I Hate New Year's Resolutions: http://www.jcdfitness.com/2012/12/forming-habits-how-i-do-it-and-why-i-hate-new-years-resolutions - Excellent article from JC Deen on how to create better habits, the problem with typical new year's resolutions, and goal setting tips that actually work.

6 Scientific Methods For Getting Motivation to Lose Weight: http://comfortpit.com/motivation-to-lose-weight - 6 scientific methods that actually work to help you lose weight. Tactic #1, doublethink, is genius. It explains how visualizing can actually be detrimental to your success unless you're doing it the right way.

Habitual Mastery: http://www.scotthyoung.com/blog/2006/05/09/ introduction-habitual-mastery-series - A great series by Scott Young on habit development using conditioning, leverage, replacement, and experimentation.

Did You Love The Healthy Habit Revolution?

Thank you for investing in yourself and in this book.

As a special reward for completing this challenge, I'm offering you a free copy of any one of my books if you email me your results. Simply shoot a message over to derek@upgradeyourhabits.com and tell me about your experience answering a few questions I have that take several minutes. Then you can claim a copy of any one of my other books.

If you enjoyed this book, please let others know how much they can benefit from it by leaving a review here: http://upgradeyourhabits.com/revolution

If you have feedback on how to make this book even better, I'd love to hear it at derek@upgradeyourhabits.com

Thanks!

Derek Doepker

Closing Thoughts

To close this book, I'd like to leave you with one of the most important concepts I've learned when it comes to improving your life, and that is this – success is about *striving*. You're going to screw up plenty of times and make a hell of a lot of mistakes, and that's OK. To this day I sometimes still find myself failing to act upon what I know I need to do, but the reason why I'm able to get out of it is because I can catch myself and get back on track.

"Courage doesn't always roar. Sometimes courage is the little voice at the end of the day that says, 'I'll try again tomorrow.'" – Mary Anne Radmacher

Knowing that you're going to get knocked down, give yourself permission to be OK with that, while making a commitment to always get back up - fast. That's all that really matters. And if you ever need a helping hand to pull yourself up, remember that I'm here for you.

Derek Doepker

References

Dana R. Carney, Amy J.C. Cuddy, Andy J. Yap. "Power Posing: Brief Nonverbal Displays Affect Neuroendocrine Levels and Risk Tolerance." *Psychological Science* (2010): 1363-1368. Web.

Moyer CA, Donnelly MP, Anderson JC, Valek KC, Huckaby SJ, Wiederholt DA, Doty RL, Rehlinger AS, Rice BL. "Frontal electroencephalographic asymmetry associated with positive emotion is produced by very brief meditation training." *Psychological Science* (2011).

Muraven, Mark, Marylène Gagné, and Heather Rosman. "Helpful Self-Control: Autonomy Support, Vitality, and Depletion." *Journal of experimental social psychology 44.3* (2008): 573-585. Web.

Taren AA, Creswell JD, Gianaros PJ. "Dispositional Mindfulness Co-Varies with Smaller Amygdala and Caudate Volumes in Community Adults." *PLoS ONE* (2013).

Vanessa M. Patrick, Henrik Hagtvedt. "'I Don't' versus 'I Can't': When Empowered Refusal Motivates Goal-Directed Behavior." *Journal of Consumer Research, Forthcoming* (2012). Available at SSRN: http://ssrn.com/abstract=2086837.

Printed in Great Britain
by Amazon